Christ's Second Coming, a Message for the Church

To Annemarie

Keep the faith to the end.

10/2/10

Christ's Second Coming, a Message for the Church

❖

The Mysteries of Spirits and Their Roles in Prophecy

Austin Phillips

Library of Congress Control Number:		2010901140
ISBN:	Hardcover	978-1-4500-3474-6
	Softcover	978-1-4500-3473-9
	Ebook	978-1-4500-3475-3

To order additional copies of this book, contact:
Xlibris Corporation
1-888-795-4274
www.Xlibris.com
Orders@Xlibris.com
73085

CONTENTS

Acknowledgement 7

Preface 9

Introduction 11

Chapter One   My Calling / Visitations from Heaven 13

Chapter Two   Who Created the Heavens and the Earth? 21

Chapter Three   Darkness Separated from Light 36

Chapter Four   Spirits Have no Flesh or Bones 41

Chapter Five   The Many Faces of Satan 52

Chapter Six   First Seal 70

Chapter Seven The Time of the End 76

Chapter Eight   Personal Revelation of the First Seal 88

Chapter Nine   Two Nations 98

Chapter Ten   Daniel's Beast Identified 105

Message to the Church 109

ACKNOWLEDGEMENT

To God be the Glory for giving me the spiritual guidance, health and wisdom to work as a servant for His Kingdom. I thank God for my wife and family as well as friends who have encouraged and supported me throughout this work.. Special thanks to Mrs. Shirley Baksh, Evelyn Williams and Eugenie Felix who assisted me in proof reading and typing. I also like to thank Jerrodoemie Winters for the illustrations and Asha Phillips for the cover design.

PREFACE

Growing up on the island of Aruba, religion and the religious community seemed to be one big family. I was not aware of any kind of divisions within the religious community on our island. I attended the Catholic church on Sundays. The priest did his ceremony, mainly in Latin, and then at times, we attended services with our neighbor who was a Seventh Day Adventist and celebrated and learned the biblical law at the Sabbath services. Another neighbor who was a Jehovah's Witness would take the children from the neighborhood to the Kingdom Hall where we participated in Bible lessons.

I also attended revivals sponsored by other congregations that seemed more traditional, and some that were Pentecostal in their beliefs. I especially liked it when the congregation would sing hymns together. Hymns like "In the Garden," "Just as I Am," and other types of closing hymns used to call sinners to repentance. I cannot recall who was sponsoring the revivals, but I considered them all Christians. My religious experiences were very positive as I was growing up, and the separation between the religious groups was not as evident then as it is today. It was a time of fellowship and learning about the Word of God.

My family moved to St. Croix just as I entered adolescence, and that is when I began to notice the division, even hostility, among Christian religious groups. It became very apparent to me after I started attending nondenominational churches. As a young man, God spoke to me and directed me to write to the various churches concerning the unity of the faith. I wrote four letters over a period of about two years, and I spoke to just about every pastor on the island of St. Croix, sharing with them what the Lord spoke to me. I was bold enough to say that God wanted the fragmented body to unite. God's message was rejected by most of the pastors; however, some pastors were polite and heard me out. Some were very candid about how they felt about the other denominations, and others were somewhat responsive to my letters and actually got together to openly discuss unity.

I did not imagine that there could be such division among those calling themselves by the name of our Lord Jesus Christ. Their division was not only in doctrine, but also in interpretation of the scriptures. Over time, the Lord comforted me from that very painful experience of telling the people of God to love each other and to function as one.

This experience was as if it were a horrific nightmare. It left me feeling confused, angry, and asking God not to have me do such a thing again. But God began to show me how he was going to bring about the unity. My job was just to tell the people what He said, and I had to learn to leave the details to Him. Getting self out of the way is a lesson that takes time, but over time, it builds faith, understanding, hope, and patience.

God will bring about the union of the faithful. He delivered to me in dreams and visions when and how. Again, following His urging, I am called to reveal those letters and the divine plan God has for accomplishing unity of the faith through the fulfilling of prophecy.

This book is one of a series of books that will be used to bring to the reader the knowledge of the intentions of God. It is a message first to the church, and then to all who would receive it. It calls attention to the prophetic word and the obedience to the teachings of the faith.

During the time of the writing of the letters, I did meet with most of the ministers, whether individually or collectively. Their response varied from passive acceptance to skepticism.

I also gave a copy of the letters to the senators and hand delivered a copy of the collection of the letters to the governor's office. I was making sure that everyone in position of leadership had a copy.

Looking back, I realized that I was hurt more because of my own ego and lack of understanding. What I expected the Lord to do was based on my personal ambition, which was getting in the way of God's plan and purpose. However, I am still learning that when I decrease, Christ increases in me. I am also gaining the proper understanding that patience is a virtue that will be learned when working for God. His ways are not like ours, nor is his purpose and plans dictated by man's schedule.

The prophetic time line is a sequence of prophetic events that will fulfill God's eternal purpose. This book is about the end result of the letters. God did exactly what God wanted to do and I was obedient in that little thing and was entrusted with this work on prophecy. I heard much, I saw much, and the revelations were in abundance. I am still learning new things, but the prophetic information clearly describes the will and purpose of God.

Now, through this work, I will share with anyone who is willing to receive what the Spirit is saying to the churches the plan of God. I have inserted a copy of the letters that were given to the ministers towards the end of the book, just before the revelations about the prophetic future of the United States. I believe the letters forewarns the Church, as well as this nation of the impending judgment, and the need to repent. The first letter is addressed to Pastor George, head of the Evangelical Ministerial Association on St. Croix. I felt led to speak to him first and share with him what was given to me.

INTRODUCTION

The pages that follow contain a message that the Lord gave me to write to the churches. This message is to call all nations to repentance and call their people to obey the teachings of this faith. It is a warning and a revelation. It is a message of hope and instruction to the born-again believer and to those individuals who have never heard the gospel of Jesus. Like the prophets Jeremiah, Habakkuk, and others before me, the Lord ordained me a prophet unto the nations. I must heed the Word of God and

> Write the vision and make it plain upon tables (books), that he may run that readeth it. For the vision is yet for an appointed time, but at the end it shall speak, and not lie: though it tarry, wait for it; because it will surely come, it will not tarry. (King James Version, Habakkuk 2:2-3)

Those words spoken to Habakkuk are relevant to me and this work today. For it is my intention, to write the vision and make it easy to be understood.

This work chronicles the vision the Lord gave to me and is my attempt to make it plain. Just as the Lord spoke to the prophet Jeremiah, my mission is to "root out, to pull down, to destroy, to throw down, to build and to plant" (KJV, Jeremiah 1:10). This book is about spirits and spiritual things. It covers areas that must be presented in order for us to study prophecy. When we read about spirits in the Bible, at times it would seem that they are the secondary entities, and man the first. We have it upside-down. They are the first, and man the secondary. Who are spirits? What are they? Where did they come from? I hope to answer those questions based on scriptural information, revelation, and personal visitations.

In this book, I describe the foundation the invisible powers that are behind the fulfillment of prophecy. The reader gets to see the different spiritual camps that affect humanity's daily life, the headquarters of the different camps, and the behavior of the people they control.

The book is about who, what, when, and how of prophecy and a must read for anyone seriously studying the subject. It also goes into detail about the spiritual roots of man, how things came about, and where we are headed and how we are to get there. It allows for a more detailed explanation of the many dreams and visions I have received, along with the revelation and interpretations. It will serve as a foundation and a reference to the books that will follow because it clearly identifies spirits and how they operate.

The Holy Bible is the only book cited, and most, if not all the quotations, are from the King James Version of the Bible. On a few occasions, liberty was taken to change a word from old English to contemporary English. The meaning of the word was not changed—just the way the word is used today was changed. An example would be changing *thou* to *you*. This was done on four or five occasions. The careful reader and serious student should be able to find the change. After carefully examining the many dreams, visions, and revelations the Lord gave to me over the last twenty years, I see how they parallel and bring clarity to the prophecies written in His Holy Word thousands of years ago. This comprehensive review is to help draw us back to God by making His Word easy to understand.

The time is at hand for this generation to see the fulfillment of all the things that were spoken through the holy apostles, prophets, and by Jesus, our Lord. Every dream, revelation, and vision that I have received, I have written and interpreted, and by the grace of God related them to the prophecies written in the scriptures. The book is therefore best read with a Bible as a companion book: the King James Version. In it, prophetic secrets and mysteries that God had hidden in the scriptures until these times, are revealed. "Those who have ears to hear will hear" what the Spirit is saying, and "those who have eyes to see will see" and understand, for surely we know that the Lord God will do nothing without first revealing it to his servants, the prophets. Amos 3:7

CHAPTER ONE

My Calling / Visitations from Heaven

God still relates to us today as he did with those before us. His Spirit is ever present, and with him, there is no variableness, neither shadow of turning (James 1:17, KJV). God has blessed mine eyes to see spirits, both good and evil, and to see angels as well as devils. Like a father who teaches his children, so the Lord has patiently instructed and guided me through many spiritual experiences and prophecies and has given me an understanding of His word.

I was awakened one night and saw what looked like a man standing at the front door inside of my room. He was fully dressed and was of average height. Everything about him was natural to my eye, yet there was something about him that was different. Not frightening, just mystical. He moved swiftly, almost at the speed of thought, stood in front of me, and greeted me with a kiss. When he kissed me, my spirit man recognized him, and rejoiced when he saw him. There was nothing perverse or unclean about him, and my spirit man began to separate from my body to greet him. Then with lightning speed, he moved back to the front of the door and sat down as if he were waiting on me.

When I came out of the vision, I wrote down all that I'd experienced. In my study of God's Word, I found that many prophets have recorded similar visits. In the scriptures, Daniel called the angel who spoke to him Gabriel. He wrote Behold, there stood before me as the appearance of a man. The angel spoke to his spirit as he did to me, for he said, "And as he was speaking with me, I was in a deep sleep on my face toward the ground: but he touched me, and set me upright. He recognized the angel from a previous vision, and said, "Yea, while I was speaking in my prayer, even the man, Gabriel, whom I had seen in the vision at the beginning, being caused to fly swiftly, touched me." (Daniel 8:15, 18; 9:21, KJV)

That same angel, Gabriel, was also sent to Zacharias to announce the coming of John the Baptist. (Luke 1:11-19). Six months later, Gabriel also appeared to Mary, the mother of our Lord, to announce the coming of Jesus Christ, the Lord (Luke 1:26-35, KJV)

The angels, who are God's messengers to man, prepare the way for God to manifest himself to those to whom He chooses to reveal Him. Soon after my first visitation, there was another vision. My spirit man (My body and my spirit were separated from each other. I call the conscious personality that exited my body the spirit man. When my body and the spirit man are united together, I am then a living soul) welcomed three spirits this time. A crystal light outlined their bodies. The three were standing, one in front of the other and appeared encased inside of what I envisioned to be an adult male. He was the tallest of the three, and the others were in the form of an adult female and a child. The male child separated himself from them and seemed to hide something in my room.

When I came out of this vision, I searched for whatever the spirit left in my room, but I did not find it. The secret was known to my spirit man but was not yet revealed to my carnal mind. During the first two visitations, no words were spoken, but from that time onward, as the Lord allowed His messengers to continue to visit me, I would hear the voices of the heavenly visitors. That time in my life afforded me an opportunity to live wholly immersed in the Word of God. My spiritual experiences progressed to the point where I would sometimes see the Spirit of God descending upon a person, and that person would bring forth the Word of the Lord.

In the beginning I did not fully understand the things of the spirit world, but as I matured in the knowledge of God's Word, spiritual things became clearer to me, and the visits by angels and by God continued.

On another occasion, I woke to hear a deep voice resonating in my hearing. It was powerful and clear like the sound of a rushing wind. It came from outside of my window, but this voice spoke words that I did not know. The deep voice was powerful and clear, but in a language that I had never heard before, a language that was profoundly different, yet my spirit rejoiced at the sound of the words, and I felt refreshed in my soul after hearing the voice.

That same day, a young man came unexpectedly to minister to me. I saw the Spirit of God descending upon him. God's spirit spoke to me through him. He spoke to me about the importance of accepting Jesus Christ as my Lord and Savior and being baptized in His Name. I always believed in Jesus, but did not understand the process of acceptance and baptism. That day, I accepted Him as Lord and Savior of my life. I was baptized in the sea, in the name of Jesus, but I still did not understand my calling or some of my experiences.

Not long after my water baptism, the Spirit led me to Miracle Revival Center Pentecostal Church in St. Croix where Luis and Virginia Ventura were the pastors. The first time I attended a service there; Pastor Virginia Ventura spoke in the language that I had heard outside of my window. I later learned from her that it was a heavenly language, a language that people filled with the Holy Ghost speak. Up until that time, I did not know that such a language existed or that it was an evidence of the Holy Ghost dwelling in our bodies. The apostle Paul, called that mystery language, unknown tongues, or tongues of angels.

In his writing to the Corinthians, he wrote, "For he that speaketh in an unknown tongue speaketh not unto men, but unto God: for no man understandeth him; howbeit in the spirit he speaketh mysteries" (1Corinthians 14:2, KJV).

Two weeks after my water baptism, I awoke from my sleep well after midnight. In the same room where I had the previous visitations sat another heavenly visitor. The light that emanated from this spirit illuminated the normally dark room. This spirit was as if light was encased in a body. The light was the color of the full moon in its brightness when it lights the earth and the sky on a clear, cloudless night. As this indescribable spirit captivated my attention, my spirit man leaped out of my body and ran toward the visitor who brought a recognizable joy to my spirit.

As I moved toward the visitor, invisible cords suddenly bound my spirit man. I could not move. The awesomeness of the visitor that sat before me literally bound my spirit man with invisible cords that surrounded my entire being. The binding was not an unpleasant experience. There was a certain majesty and power about the visitor and a calmness of deep peace that I felt in the visitor's presence and my spirit rejoiced in the presence of this glorious majesty. This visit led me to a study about how spirits could be bound and loosened. I learned that both the spirit man and the natural man are conscious. I learned that we live in different realms. Each realm has different laws and powers that govern its existence. God gives man the power and ability to live, to walk and to rule in both realms (Matthew 16:19 KJV).

As I continued to engage in fellowship with the Pentecostal believers, I saw a completely different side to the church. I saw the manifestation of the "power of the Holy Ghost." I realized that God was teaching me the reality of His word (Mark 16:17-18KJV). These activities offered a sharp contrast to the experiences I held from my Roman Catholic upbringing.

As a child, I always wanted to be a priest because I liked how they performed their services. The priest stood with outstretched arms, submitted staunch genuflections, and performed services in Latin. I did not understand what they were doing, but it was impressive to me.

Conversely, the Pentecostal services were in English, the preaching was a fiery condemnation against sin, and I saw the mighty power of God working through his servants with miracles, healings, and the casting out of devils. I heard people prophesying in tongues, and others interpreting what they said. Those experiences strengthened my belief in God whom I really wanted to know, and who had opened my eyes, showing me that his Word was truth.

Strange New Experiences: Unwelcome Spirits

With all of those spiritual experiences, there was still an unanswered question that weighed heavy in my soul. What was happening to me? Why was I hearing and seeing things that others did not hear or see? I needed to know more about God and the spiritual realm to which I was introduced. I began smoking marijuana while earnestly seeking answers and hoping to strengthen my relationship with God. During this brief period, I often smoked marijuana and read books on herbs while seeking a natural path to God. I later learned that marijuana is a unique herb and attracts spirits. I say that to emphasize that the baptism of the Holy Ghost should be sought after by every believer so as not to be tricked by other spirits. Marijuana is not a link to Jesus, but rather a link to spirits of the world whose satisfaction is in the flesh and whose end is destruction. Hopefully, by sharing this experience, I might save some from the road that leads to destruction and bondage.

Spiritual experiences under the influence of marijuana can, at times, be deceptive and mislead those who are, like I was at that time, lacking in scriptural and spiritual understanding. The scriptures teach us that people err in vision because of strong drink, and marijuana is as strong of an intoxicant as any drink. I found this to be true in my experiences as well. From as far back as I can remember, I would have dreams and visions, and all, or part of my vision and dreams would actually happen the next day, or shortly thereafter. However, the influence of marijuana skewed the way I interpreted the visions I received. The gifts of the spirit operate whether you are sober or high. Smoking marijuana at times has caused me to err in vision and judgment. I made unwise choices in my personal life, based upon erroneous interpretations. This however did not affect the prophetic word given to me, but showed me the depth of my ignorance about spirits.

"But they also have erred through wine, and through strong drink are out of the way; the priest and the prophet have erred through strong drink, they are swallowed up of wine, they are out of the way through strong drink; they err in vision, they stumble in judgment." (Isaiah 28:7, KJV)

I was having dreams and visions before smoking marijuana so this brief isolated incident only added to my experience in the spirit realm. Studying and reading the Bible under this influence was a very deceptive practice. God does not need us to use external support, such as marijuana in order for Him to speak to us and for us to interpret the dreams or visions. The Holy Ghost is the one who reveals the mysteries.

One negative spiritual experience I had while under the influence of marijuana troubled me for many years. It happened early one morning as I was sitting outside of my home in Monbijou, St. Croix. This was a different house from where I had received the previous visitations. I was meditating about life, the reasons why things happen the way they do, and enjoying the sight of the moon and its light.

I was smoking marijuana earlier that evening, but I do not believe I was under the influence of marijuana at that moment. As I sat there, I saw a spirit in the form of a child at my gate. The gate was open, and I could see the outline of his body as he stood about thirty yards away from me. I curiously watched as the spirit came toward me. I heard a voice inside of me saying, "Don't be afraid, and let him come." As the spirit drew nearer and nearer to me, it grew and grew until from a child it grew into the height of a man. Then when it was my height and standing directly in front of me, it became one with me by walking into my body. There was no great shaking or any dramatic external transformation in me. Having experienced the Spirit of God descending upon me in the past, I was not alarmed, but this experience was different because the Spirit grew from a child as I was watching it, and then walked into me. I always believed that God would deliver me from any evil, so I was not afraid of the spirit, and I was really thinking that it was the Spirit of God.

The next day while riding the bus, a young boy saw me and got all excited and began to tell his mom that I was the man he saw. I reasoned that he dreamt about me because I had never seen the youth before that day, yet I was somehow communicating with the child. Without saying a word, I knew his thoughts. When I went to church that night, there was a discussion on the nature of God, and I spoke boldly concerning some things I had seen before. I spoke concerning the male and female nature of God I had seen in one of my previous visitations. That information was not well received. Members of the congregation criticized me for what the Lord had shown me; they called me crazy, and I was firmly rebuked.

During that service, a young girl stood up and said she had a dream about me the night before. In her dream, it was revealed to her that I was telling her "It was God." I did not reveal to the congregation what happened to me early that morning as I myself was still trying to understand it. I left the service that night bewildered and deeply disappointed at the reaction of my pastor and the congregation elders. So I kept my most recent experience to myself. "But there is a God in heaven who gives dreams, and seals our instructions in the night when deep sleeps fall upon us" (Job 33:14-15 (KJV).

The spirit that came into me taught me a lesson about spirits and how they can mislead and destroy those lacking knowledge of the scriptures. After a while, I found myself unable to stop smoking marijuana. I would smoke it and pick up my Bible to read, but I could not read it or study as I used to in the past. I found myself driven by the desire to get high. When I would get high, a spirit of darkness took over my body. I became a different person. At times, it took me where I did not know I was going. I would get in my car and end up in strange places, oftentimes unable to find my way home. It was as if the spirit that inhabited me at that time was trying to learn what I already knew. There was nothing holy about that spirit—by their fruits, you shall know them (Matthew 12:33, KJV)—and I began losing rather than gaining because of it.

At first I believed that it was the Spirit of God and my friends and family members had wrongly rejected me. However, after a while I began to pray and asked God to take it away. Soon thereafter, my marriage fell apart, and I could not get or keep a job. One day, while praying earnestly and asking God to take that spirit from me, I was reading the book of Psalms and I felt that spirit of darkness leave. It took me a while before I understood the lesson that God was teaching me, but I am sure that it was not only a lesson for me, but others as well.

Lessons Learned

There are spirits that possess the body and control it. Marijuana is an herb that opens the door for those kinds of spirits. We must be aware that some of those spirits can mislead the curious. Every believer should be part of a body of believers where there are elders and pastors who are filled with the Holy Ghost and can discern spirits and deliver those who are bound by unholy spirits. Unclean spirits and spirits of darkness are real, and those spirits are behind the grief that is disrupting many homes, communities, and individual lives.

The Spirit of God does not lead to sin, but leads us away from sin. I devoted an entire section on spiritual warfare to show how to overcome the spirits that invade our homes and lives. I thank God for the experience because now I know not only from reading, but also from experience. The only reason I discussed these experiences is to give others an example of the ignorance that destroys babes in Christ: those new to His Word and His way. I drifted to the use of marijuana because there were unanswered questions about my prophetic visions, my dreams and my gift from God. The lack of spiritual guidance early in my church life left me vulnerable and confused.

In retrospect, I know that God never stopped guiding me by His spirit, but the only way I could get a better understanding was to have someone mature in the truth of spiritual things teach me. God taught me through those experiences as I was guided in the reality of His Word. The prophet Isaiah boldly declares, "Whom shall he teach knowledge? Or whom shall he make to understand doctrine? Them that are weaned from the milk, and drawn from the breast" (Isaiah 28:9, KJV).

Growth in His Word

After that experience I left the island of St. Croix. Hurricane Hugo had left the economy and communities of St. Croix in ruins and I needed to be with my family. About twenty years after the first visit by the Spirit of God, I was meditating and reading the Bible on the campus of Deeper Life Church in Tampa, Florida, where I was attending the school of ministry. Deeper Life is a deliverance and faith-building church where Bishop Jefferson is the founding pastor. He boldly offers the spiritual guidance and instructions that feed those who earnestly seek to grow in Christ. He also teaches the necessity of being filled with the Holy Ghost. I found that environment to be the ideal place for me to cultivate a deeper walk with God.

Before going to Deeper Life, the power of God was demonstrated in my life by casting out devils, laying hands on the sick and seeing them recover, but it was not until I was a student at Deeper Life that I received the evidence of the Holy Ghost by the gift of speaking in tongues. Someone out there might have a gift or gifts from God and are not speaking in tongues. Don't be discouraged. If this is your desire, ask God for the gift of tongues, but remember that Paul said he prefers that you prophesy to the edifying of the church than to speak in unknown tongues (1 Corinthians 14:5, KJV).

Bishop Jefferson and his wife compel their members to live a clean and holy life, to pray, fast, and study the Bible. God had opened a dream door for me. I had the time to write and meditate upon the Lord and His Word. Deeper Life Ministries offered an environment that was very conducive to this spiritual work, and I was learning and growing. One morning around ten while studying on the grounds, I saw an angel on the sidewalk that runs east of the church and the compound. This angel was bigger in size and was more physically developed than the one I had previously seen in my room in St. Croix.

The angel had a sickle in his hand and was walking on the sidewalk in front of the church. The angel's color was different from the one who had visited me before, for he had long locks on his head while the other angel's head was covered. (I suppose this is why Paul said, "For this cause ought the woman to have power on her head because of the angels" [1Corinthians 11:10, KJV].)

He walked in front of the church on the paved sidewalk, and then he stopped, turned, and looked at me. He paused for a moment as if he was waiting for me, then he vanished. This visit brought great joy to me because it was the first visitation I had while studying at Deeper Life.

I took note, however, that the Lord had sent his messenger to prepare his way. For not long after that, while reading the book of Ephesians, I was sitting at the very spot where I saw the angel. Standing about thirty feet from me, I saw a woman whom I had seen before in a dream coming to visit me. In the dream, I was told her name is Jehovah. The light around her was bright, and from the distance, I could see her silver white hair, but her face was not discernable. Her clothing was white and a light blue mix, giving it a blue sky color, and she wore a golden belt around her waist. She stood on the grounds of the churchyard, looked at me for a moment, and then vanished. Her presence humbled my spirit within me and brought me great joy as it did when I had the heavenly visitor in my room, which had demonstrated to me the power to bind and to loose the spirits.

On another occasion, while praising God during praise and worship service, having mine eyes closed, I felt someone touch me upon the shoulder. As I opened mine eyes, I saw the same woman with her back facing me standing in front of me. As soon as I saw her, she vanished from my sight. I recognized her as Jehovah, the third person in the Godhead, the one who had visited me in my visions and dreams while in St. Croix, giving me the lesson on binding/loosening spirits, and more recently when I relocated to Tampa. God came to encourage me to act within my calling from God to "write the vision" and to tell of all of the things that I have both seen and heard from God.

CHAPTER TWO

Who Created the Heavens and the Earth?

This book's main focus is about spirits and spiritual things. It covers spiritual entities that must be presented in order for us to understand and study prophecies. When we read about spirits in the Bible, at times, it would seem that they are the secondary entities, man being the first. That is an upside-down view. Before the creation of man, spirits in their purest form existed. Man was given a spirit and then became a living soul.

A place was created just for spirits who have no body, and a place was created for those with a body. Then there are those who go from body to body, seeking a place of rest or refuge. So what or who are spirits? God is a spirit, and every creature enclosed in flesh has a spirit. Where did spirits come from? Spirits come from God who is the Father of spirits. I hope to confirm those statements using the scriptures as a guide, as well as divine revelation and personal visitations.

The best place to begin this journey is the book of Genesis, beginning with the history of creation. "These are the generations of the heavens and of the earth when they were created in the day that the Lord God made the earth and the heavens, and every plant of the field before it was in the earth, and every herb of the field before it grew: for the Lord God had not caused it to rain upon the earth, and there was not a man to till the ground." Gen: 2:4.

In the beginning of the creation of the heavens and earth, according to the scriptures, waters that covered the face of the deep. The earth, as we know it, was without shape and form because it was loose particles in the waters. The waters that covered the face of the deep was not simply H2O, but something I will call the "Living Gel," for lack of a better word. It was shown to me as a black substance that quivered and moved like the deep waters of the ocean that looks solid, but is constantly moving. Whatever that substance was, it had the necessary mixture of things needed to create living things. No doubt it was filled with innumerable combinations of irons, atoms, different elements, and gases. There was the potential for life, but it needed a designer and a creator to set in motion a perfectly calculated series of events, which the scriptures refer to as creation.

The life-giving energy of God moved upon the face of the "waters" causing a powerful explosive phenomenon, and God said, "Let there be light and there was light, and God saw that the light was good and separated the light from the darkness. And the evening and the morning were the first day." (Gen.1:2). That light must be understood as literal, a source of energy powerful enough to separate the darkness from light and placing in the universe somewhere a permanent fixture of energy in the form of light. It was also powerful enough to separate the body of waters; hurling half of it far into the heavens, and the other half we enjoy on earth as the seas, rivers and lakes. Searching the surrounding planets would undoubtedly reveal the existence of water out of which the solid or combinations of elements was formed, or the water had contact with them on its way through space. I suppose just as there is the sun in our solar system, there exist similar lights in other planetary system. Not much else is mentioned about the creation of the heavens and their life forms in the book of Genesis account of creation; however, references about the existence of celestial creatures and other worlds are made throughout the scriptures. (Gen 1:8-26).

The light or the energy that was released by God is also figuratively described as the beginning of the creation of God, Jesus, the son of God. "By him all things were made, and without him was not anything made that was made." That light is called the Son of God who was with God from the beginning of creation. He was separated from the darkness that God called the Night, and the light he called the Day. (Rev.3:14, John 1:1-5, Heb1:2). This is not the light of the sun and the moon that supports life on earth, but the light that will light the New Jerusalem when it comes down from heaven. Rev. 22:5.That light is the spiritual light of heaven that lights the godly man on earth.

The creation of the heavens and heavenly things took place over several generations as we read. How long is a creation generation with God? I do not know, however, it consisted of the evening and the morning. God worked for six days and the seventh day was a day of rest. The first generational period ended with the Light separating from Darkness. I believe that during that generational period there was a separation of the different kinds of spirits. Those that are of the Night have a different personality from those of the day. God saw the light that it was good and God separated the light from the darkness." Also, God said, "I form the light, and create darkness: I make peace and create evil: I the Lord do all these things." Isa. 45:7. Their good or evil natures were natural to them in their own habitat.

On the second day of creation, there was the separation of the universal waters, which was to create separate worlds. "And God made a firmament, and divided the waters which were under the firmament from the waters which were above the firmament . . . God called the firmament heaven. And the evening and the morning were the second day." (Gen 1:8). So there is water above our solar system and water on earth. The worlds above our solar system the Bible refers to as the heavens, or heaven. The prophet David, in songs of praise to God, commanded the heavenly creation to praise their creator, saying: "Praise ye the Lord. Praise ye the Lord from the heavens: praise him in the heights. Praise ye him, sun and moon: praise him, all his angels: praise ye him, all his host. Praise ye him, sun and moon: praise him, all ye stars of light. Praise him, ye heavens of heavens, and ye waters that be above the heavens. Let them praise the name of the Lord for he commanded and they were created. He hath also established them forever and ever; he hath made a decree which shall not pass." Psalms 148:1-6.

Just as sure as the sun and the moon and the stars are in their place, so also is there a place outside of our solar system that is filled with water and celestial creatures to numerous to mention. Water is a life-giving source and just like on earth where we find water, we will find a host of creatures who enjoys its life sustaining benefits. God through His life-giving energy was in full control of the events taking place and thus continued the creation of celestial life. Spirits were given bodies and assigned places to live. (Gen. 1:3-13, Heb1:2, 7). The life forms that were created in heaven were called by different names including: angels, the Morning Stars, the sons of God, and Satan, to name a few, as well as other living creatures whose life energy (spirit) emanated from the Spirit of God. These all worshipped and served God and helped in the creation of the universe.

The Creators

It is written that Jesus, "Is the image of the invisible God, the firstborn of every creature. For by him were all things created, that are in heaven, and that are in earth, visible and invisible, whether they be thrones, or dominions, or principalities, or powers: all things were created by him and for him." Col.1:15-16. John wrote that all things were made by the Word, which became flesh, which was with God from the beginning, and was God. "Without him was not anything made, that was made." (John 1:3).

From the very beginning God, Father, Son, and Mother, were working together. The Mother, who is also known as wisdom, was there from the beginning. She is the Spirit that rested on Jesus when he was baptized in the Jordan River and anointed to preach and do the work His Father sent him to do on earth. "And the Spirit of the Lord shall rest upon him, the Spirit of wisdom and understanding, the Spirit of counsel and might, the Spirit of Knowledge and of the fear of the Lord" (Isa.11:2). Jesus' Mother remained with Him up to his crucifixion on the cross. John 19:26-30. Jesus himself bore witness to the Spirit of God being upon him and enabling him to do the work he was sent to do on earth (Lu 4:18-19).

King Solomon highlighted the role of wisdom in his writing on the creation. He wrote of wisdom: "The Lord possessed me in the beginning of his way, before his works of old. I was set up from everlasting, from the beginning, or ever the earth was. When there were no depths, I was brought forth; when there were no fountains abounding with water. Before the mountains were settled, before the hills was I brought forth: While as yet he had not made the earth, or the fields, or the highest part of the dust of the world. When he prepared the heavens, I was there: when he set a compass upon the face of the depth: When he established the clouds above: when he strengthened the fountains of the deep: When he gave to the sea his decree, that the waters should not pass his commandment: when he appointed the fountain of the earth; Then I was by Him, as one brought up with Him, and I was daily His delight, rejoicing always before Him." (Prov. 8:22-30)

Then from the book of Job, God asked a rhetorical question, "Where were thou when I laid the foundation of the earth? Declare if thou hast understanding. Who had laid the measures thereof if thou knowest? Or who has stretched the line upon it? Where upon are the foundations thereof fastened? Or who laid the corner stone thereof: when the morning star sang together and all the sons of God shouted for joy? (Job 38:4-7). The answer supports the statement that Wisdom and Her children were there working along with the Father in the creation of the universe. The universe and all its host grace and mystery clearly points to a divine creator. The heavens declare the glory of God and the firmament sheweth his handiwork Psalms 19:1, wrote the Psalmist. The harmony, consistency, overall beauty of what we see, hear, and feel, is not accidental, but shows forth the glory, the majesty, and the wisdom of the Godhead.

Paradise

There exists a land where the light it receives has nothing to do with our solar system. It is another planet just like the earth, situated on another world called Paradise. Many structures and things associated with religious life was patterned after things in heaven. Man will continue to advance in knowledge and wisdom and acquire skills needed for the betterment of human life. Yet man's greatest technological achievements will never rival those of his celestial counterparts. The inspired wisdom on earth comes from the divine Spirit of God, who gives man the wisdom to create a better world, like the one from which original man was cast out. The apostle Paul was taken into that place where he said, "I was caught up into Paradise where he heard unspeakable words, which is not lawful for a man to utter." The location of that place he said was in the third heaven (2Cor: 12:2, 4). There in the midst of the Paradise of God is the tree of life (Rev.2:7).

Paradise is not an imaginary place where a person's spirit enters after they die. It is a land filled with innumerable creatures, and angels and the spirits of just men made perfect as written in the book of Hebrews: "But ye are come unto mount Zion, and unto the city of the living God, the heavenly Jerusalem, and to an innumerable company of angels. To the general assembly and church of the firstborn, which are written in heaven, and to God the judge of all, and to the spirits of just men, made perfect, and to Jesus, the mediator of the new covenant, and to the blood of sprinkling that speaketh better things than that of Abel" (Heb. 12:22-24).

The apostle John was taken to heaven in the spirit and was given a tour of this great city. This is what he wrote about his experience. "And immediately I was in the Spirit: and behold, a throne was set in heaven, and one sat on the throne. And he that sat was to look upon like jasper and a sardine stone: and there was a rainbow round about the throne, in sight like unto an emerald." Heaven is a kingdom where the King of Kings lives. There is more: "And round about the throne were four and twenty seats: and upon the seats I saw four and twenty elders sitting, clothed in white raiment, and they had on their heads crowns of gold." These are the spirits of just men made perfect (see Revelation5:9-10). "And before the throne there was a sea of glass like unto a crystal. And in the midst of the throne, and round about the throne, were four beasts full of eyes before and behind." [I described those in more detail in another chapter.] "And I beheld, and, lo, in the midst of the throne and of the four beast, and in the midst of the elders, stood a Lamb as it had been slain, having seven horns and seven eyes, which are the seven Spirits of God sent into all the earth." The Lamb is Jesus, the mediator between God and man. "And I beheld, and I heard the voice of many angels round about the throne, and the beast, and the elders: and the number of them was ten thousand times ten thousand and thousands of thousands" (Rev.4:3-6, 5:6, 11).

When we multiply thousands times thousands and then multiply that by thousands times thousands, we end up with a big number. These are the innumerable company of angels who make up the armies of God. I don't think all who live there sit around heaven all day doing nothing. These are the ones that are actively engaged in the daily operations and administration of life throughout the universe. John also saw creatures, animals of all sorts. "Every creature which is in heaven" (Rev.5:13). They were too much to describe except in one word.

Just as there are terrestrial bodies, so likewise these are celestial. Those that live in Paradise and in the heavens are celestial and are subject to the celestial laws that govern such bodies. On that planet are streams of water, rivers, and oceans. There are trees and green fields and other material elements found on earth. There exists a civilization that far exceeds ours, and it is the source of wisdom and inspiration for man's advancement.

The Psalmist referred to the manna that the Israelites once ate; according to the scriptures, the corn from heaven. "Though he commanded the clouds from above, and open the doors from heaven, and rained down manna upon them to eat, and had given them of the corn of heaven. Man did eat angels' food" (Psalms 78:23-25). The manna tasted like honey wafers and coriander seed. Here again, things that we can relate to on earth is found in Paradise.

Personal Revelations

The Lord showed me the planet that I saw after I was taken into heaven. First I had to travel through a dark empty place in the sky beyond the visible stars. After the dark place, I saw a land with green fields. The grass was very green and the land looked well watered. There was a river running through the land, and its water was very clean. It was crystal clear. Now Paradise is in heaven, but it does not occupy all of heaven. I must share this revelation when writing about Paradise because in another revelation about heaven, I saw it as a world that looked like earth. The two were very similar in appearance as if one was a prototype of the other. The light from the heavenly planet was brighter than the light on the earth. The heavenly planet also had a golden city surrounded by light. The continents were divided on the planet I saw, and the celestial creatures lived in their respective place. There were buildings and a city surrounded by a high wall. There was also another place in heaven that looked like a dark sea with the surface looking like glass. Heaven is a world. Paradise is a place in heaven that God has set aside for those who are redeemed by Jesus who said: "I am going to prepare a place for you . . . In my Father's house there are many mansions." John 14:2

In another dream I was taken to place where I saw different kinds of creatures, and it was told to me in the dream that there are seven heavens. Some of the places that were inhabited looked barren, having no vegetation. The amounts or level of heavens I cannot write about with any biblical evidence to support other than Paul writing that he was caught up to the third heaven, and the Psalmist writing about the heavens of heavens. I feel that I should share that revelation because to me it only deepens the mystery of God and the unsearchable depths of God's creation.

The Creation of Earth

After creating the heavenly paradise, God proceeded to create the earth. The original earth was not as we know it today. Over a period of time and divine intervention and manipulation, the earth evolved into what it is today. The life forms on earth we know by various names: including: man, animals, fishes, birds, bacteria, insects, and other living organism to numerous to mention. Gen. 1:20-28

I want to emphasize that the days of creation are not lunar days. During the first three days of creation, there was neither sun, nor moon, to measure time as we know it. "And God said let the waters under the heaven be gathered together unto one place, and let the dry land appear: and it was so. And God called the dry land Earth; and the gathering together of the waters called the Seas: and God saw that it was good. And God said, Let the earth bring forth grass, the herb yielding seed, and the fruit tree yielding fruit after his kind, whose seed is in itself upon the earth: and it was so . . . And the evening and the morning were the third day. Gen; 1-13.

The solar system was not yet in place in place, but the earth was filled with vegetation that was able to produce seeds after its kind. Those plants and trees took a while to grow and produce seed. Within that generation, the earth, which appeared after the receding of the waters and the settling of the particles that make up our planet, was able to bring forth the necessary food source for creatures not yet created. God in his infinite wisdom knew exactly what was needed for: birds, fishes, animals, insects, and humans to flourish on earth.

Our solar system came on the fourth day when God said: "Let there be lights in the firmament of the heavens to divide the day from the night; and let them be for signs, and for seasons, and for days, and years: and let them be for lights in the firmament of the heaven to give light upon the earth: and it was so. And God made two great light . . . he made the stars also. And God set them in the firmament of the heaven to give light upon the earth. And to rule over the day and over the night and to divide the light from the darkness . . . And the evening and the morning were the fourth day." Gen.1:14. Those lights we know as the sun and moon which we associate with our solar system. From these we calculate hours and months and years. However, the earth was teeming with life long before these were created

Creation Shows God's Glory

Figuratively speaking, the two lights also represent the divine image of God as a family consisting of male and female, and the stars represent children. The apostle Paul in writing about that natural order of procreation wrote to the Romans saying: For the invisible things of him from the creation of the world are clearly seen, being understood by the things that are made, even his eternal power and Godhead, so that they are without excuse. Rom.1:20. The Psalmist also alludes to creation showing the image of the Godhead. He wrote, "The heavens declare the glory of God and the firmament showed forth his handy works" (Psalms 19:1). When we look into the sky, we see the sun, moon, and stars. These are described as the father, mother, and children in the scriptures. Joseph, the son of Jacob, dreamed about those elements.

Joseph saw in his dream the sun and the moon and the stars making obeisance unto him. When he told his father the dream, his father rebuked him saying, "Shall I and thy mother and thy brethren indeed come and bow down to thee" (Gen 37:10). Throughout creation, we find a consistent pattern affirming the naturalness of the family consisting of male and female who are charged to replenish the earth.

There was a time when it did not rain on the earth, but a mist went up from the ground to water the earth. Out of that life producing substance, God called forth and created the living creatures, as we read from the book of Genesis: "These are the generations of the heavens and the earth when they were created in the day that the Lord God made the earth and the heavens. And every plant of the field before it was in the earth, and every herb of the field before it grew: for the Lord God had not caused it to rain upon the earth, and there was no man to till the ground. But there went up a mist from the earth, and watered the whole face of the ground" (Gen.2:4-5). From that evolving process, the earth and its life forms progress to what we see and know today. Our forefathers lived on a different earth, with different atmospheric conditions.

The Creation of Man

The question of where did man come from and where he is going no doubt has crossed many minds. I do not have the answer to those questions, but I have some information that might shed some light According to the Bible, humans are in the express image and likeness of God who created them: "And God said, let us make man in our image, after our likeness . . . So God created man in his own image, in the image of God created he him; male and female created he them . . . And called their name Adam in the day when they were created" (Gen. 1:26, 5:2). The man and the woman were created to look like God. The invisible was made visible for all to see. The following revelation I received in a dream that relates to the creation of man.

I saw a substance, for lack of a better descriptive word, I will call, the "living gel." It was black, and it moved when slightly shaken, quivering like a living mass. I suppose it was a collection of living cells, but without any particular form or shape. Then I saw a spirit in the form of a man enter into the gel. When the spirit came out of the gel, it had flesh upon it, and it looked like a man. The man was alone, and then the spirit that brought forth the man entered into the man who looked like he became pregnant. Then out of the man was brought forth a woman who was of a lighter complexion than the man. That is what I saw in relation to the creation of man.

The process of creation of man and every other living creature came about after the Spirit of God moved upon the face of the waters and spoke the word. Let there be light. This was followed by God separating the waters into heaven and earth. God then brought forth life forms out of the living water and out of the dry land which he caused to appear. Man was created out of a mixture of water and earth (Gen. 2:6). The earth-and-water combination (at the time man was formed, there was a mist that watered the earth) formed into the shape of a body was not conscious, but merely a collection of cells formed into organs, and tissues. It was not until God breathed into the body the breath of life that the man became a living soul. The flesh of the man and the woman were both in the shape and likeness of the Spirits who created them and designed to house the spirits that would inhabit them. The physical man on a cellular level has everything in common with other creatures formed out of the living earth. In the book of Psalms, the writer wrote, "Thou sendest forth thy spirit, they are created: and thou renewest the face of the earth." Psalms 104:30

Every creature that has flesh also received a spirit from God. Solomon made very clear the difference between man and beast when he wrote: All go unto one place; all are of the dust, and all return to dust again. Who knoweth the spirit of man that goeth upward and the spirit of the beast that goeth downward to the earth? Ecc.3:20-21. We both decay. However, man was the Holy Spirit which elevated him above the beast. He was also given the capacity to learn, to create and to subdue the earth because he was the son of God.

Our House

The human body, according to Job, is simply a house for the spirit in which God allows us to live on this earth for a season of time. "How much less in them that dwell in houses of clay, whose foundation is in the dust", wrote Job . . . "Thou hast clothed me with skin and flesh, and hast fenced me with bones and sinews" (Job 4:19, 10:11). This brings up the question. How many bodies did God form out of the dust of the earth? The first man who was created was spirit in the likeness of God. Then the body was formed to be inhabited by the spirit. My conclusion is that many were formed and few were taken into the garden to dwell amongst the other creatures formed by God. Those taken into Eden were called Adam and given dominion over the earth, and over those who were not elevated by God through his Holy Spirit. The Father and Mother sent forth in the flesh, spirits who bore their image, the children of light. God also send forth in the flesh, the image of the spirits of the Darkness. God separated to two and they were to have no relationship with each other.

A good example of these two camps is found in the story of Cain and Abel. Cain, who is referred to as belonging to the wicked one, (1Jn 3:12), was Eves' first born son. She referred to him as," a man from the Lord." He killed his brother Abel out of envy. After God, not his parents, confronted Cain for the murder of his brother, God said to Cain, "And now thou art cursed from the earth, which hath opened her mouth to receive thy brother's blood from thy hand. When thou tillest the ground, it shall not henceforth yield unto thee her strength; a fugitive and a vagabond shalt thou be in the earth. Cain was concerned that anyone finding him would slay him, so God set a mark upon Cain to protect him. Then Cain went out from the presence of God and dwelt in the land of Nod. From there he started a lineage which no longer fellowshipped with God. Gen.4:10-16.

After a hundred and thirty years on the earth, Eve conceived again and called her son Seth," For God, said she had given me another seed instead of Abel whom Cain slew. Then in the days of Seth's son Enos, men began to call on the name of the Lord. Gen.4:25-26. What were they doing during the years in between? Seth was born in the image and likeness of Adam, who was in the image and likeness of God. From Seth, the posterity of Adam is listed. The Bible is a history and prophetic destiny of the children of light. These are the children God continuously visits, redeems and to whom He has given hope. In the listing of the genealogy of Jesus, Adam is listed as the Son of God: "Adam who was the Son of God" (Luke 3:38), from whom Jesus descended. The writer of the book of Hebrews lists God as our spiritual father, "Furthermore, we have the fathers of our flesh who corrected us, and to whom we gave the reverence: shall we not much rather be in subjection unto the Father of Spirits, and live?" (Hebrews 12:9). The apostle James refers to God as the Father of lights (Jm 1:17). These two spiritual camps were separated on the first day of creation. Adam also called his wife Eve "because she was the mother of all living" (Gen.3:20). God is the God of all spirits and the creator of flesh (Jer. 32:27). That body, and the body, Eve, who were created in the image and likeness of the invisible God were given the charge to populate the earth. Flesh had one thing in common, blood. From that one blood, the human race was made. (Acts 17:26).

God called the male and the female Adam. The man called the female woman because, he said," she was taken out of man". Therefore shall a man leave his mother and father and cleave unto his wife: and they shall be one flesh" (Genesis 2:23-24). The union of the flesh made them one. In Christ we become one Spirit when we are joined to his Spirit. The apostle Paul used the allegory of Christ and the church to point to a mystery that was not fully revealed. This mystery I believe has to do with the body of believers being called by one name.

After Adam fell from his exalted position and was driven from the presence of God: God said, "And I will be a Father unto you and ye shall be my sons and daughters, saith the Lord Almighty" (2 Corinthians 6:18). Fallen man who was created in the image of God through the grace of God is now able to be reunited into the family of God by the renewing of the Spirit of God into the temple of man. "What know ye not that your body is the temple of the Holy Ghost which is in you, which ye have of God, and ye are not your own (1Cor. 6:19)?

The mind poisoned by the knowledge of evil must also be renewed and the body must be brought into subjection to the laws of God. Then guided by the Holy Spirit and the knowledge of truth, man is restored back to the divine nature. In his divine state, man, through the Spirit of God, is not limited in what he can do. Jesus told his disciples if they believe, nothing will be impossible to them that believe. Mt. 17:20. The man Jesus, who was the expressed image of the Father, came to show us to the spiritual image of God, which the life of sin distorted beyond recognition.

The Effects of Sin in the Flesh

The human body is a collection of cells that forms tissues and organs. Those cells, at one point in time before sin entered the world, had an immortal gene code. That code was removed, and a new code, which programmed the body to die, entered the human gene pool. The human flesh became subject to death and decay and the knowledge to eternal life was hidden from man and closely guarded by the angels with flaming swords (Gen.3:23-24). Man in this sinful flesh retained his creative genius, and the ability to seek out and find out things that can benefit him and humanity. God inspires man to seek out his works as is written, "He hath made everything beautiful in his time: also he hath set the world in their heart, so that no man can find out the work that God maketh from the beginning to the end" (Eccl. 3:11). Man will come up with scientific and medical breakthroughs to help his ailing flesh. He will write laws to govern his unruly fellow humans and curiously raise many questions. He will invent great and foolish things. Yet he will never find out in its totality, the creation secrets that remain with God.

The breath of Life

The spirit in man is the breath of God and referred to as the heart. The spirit in man can be desperately wicked and filled with evil according to Jeremiah (17:9-10) Jesus said that out of the heart (spirit) proceeds evil thought and murders, fornications, and other such evils. The spirit within us lusted to envy, according to James. The spirit uses the body to fulfill the desires of the spirit and the flesh. The body is also alive with natural cravings for basic needs. The soul, or the mind, refers to that consciousness where desires are filtered and decisions are made, good or bad. Information helps determine our choices, and shows our wisdom or our stupidity.

The spirit is subject to influences from spirits, good or bad. Those filled with the Spirit of God are infused with certain gifts and knowledge that they can only receive from God and are in communication with God. Then there are those that occupy themselves with occult knowledge and receive knowledge from the spirits of darkness. The body and the mind are constantly presented with information that bring them into subjection to one of the two spiritual camps.

After the fall of Man

Most parents, when confronted with the separation from their children, will do whatever is necessary to save them or restore the broken relationship. Having lost their children to sin and death, God, as loving parents, found a way through the second Adam (Jesus and church). We are God's offspring as Paul told the Athenians, "Forasmuch then as we are the offspring of God," (Acts17:29), and he loves us. After separation from God in the Garden of Eden, and his return to earth, man's influences came mainly from the spirits of darkness. The seed of the serpent prospered in the earth, and we read that their works and imaginations were only to do evil. God repented that he made man and destroyed the world with the flood. (Gen 6:)

God, however, had given the woman a seed whose nature was like his. Evil continued to be in the earth even after the destruction of all humans, except Noah and his children, because the spirit of evil that occupies the flesh was not destroyed in the flood. The seed of the woman is distinguishable from the seed of the serpent by their works, just as light is distinguishable from darkness, are we able to recognize them. The epic struggle continues with light fighting against darkness, good versus evil.

Therefore, we must not only put away the filth of the flesh, but also of the spirit, as we perfect holiness in the fear of God. (2 Cor. 7:1) God requires that we submit our spirits in faith to his Word. So in the flesh man continued to replenish the earth, but a spirit other than God's was also multiplying in the earth.

The First Family

The mystery of the Godhead is revealed through creation. God is a Holy Family from where all spirits of light have their beginning. Paul wrote, "For this cause I bow my knees unto the Father of our Lord Jesus Christ, of whom the whole family in heaven and earth is named" (Eph.3:14-15). Adam was told to replenish the earth. God confirmed that they came from a father and mother when He said, "Therefore shall a man leave his father and mother and cleave to his wife," when there was no one else for them to leave but God. That command makes marriage honorable in all things, and the bed undefiled (Heb.13:4) "so that a man who is joined to a wife should not be ashamed" (Gen. 2:25).

The family on earth is patterned after the family in heaven, and it was and is established by God. A child is the genetic makeup of male and female, the parent's egg and seed. That is why God said, "Honor thy Father and Mother that thy days may be long upon the land which the Lord thy God giveth thee" (Ex. 20:12). For those who will not honor their parents, I have one thing to say, you are ungrateful and deserving of death. You could not have been born into this world without your parents. The saints have a Mother and Father whose throne is in heaven. This we also know from the book of Malachi; "And did not he make one? Yet had he the residue of the Spirit. And wherefore one? That he might seek a godly seed. Therefore take heed to your spirit, and let none deal treacherously against the wife of his youth" (Mal. 2:15). The man and woman who bring such an understanding into their marriage will have an enduring marriage.

Another example of how God saw the two as one was when they were judged by God (in the Garden of Eden). God judged them as one and called them man. After their sentence was handed down, we read, "And the Lord said, Behold, the man is become as one of us, [God indicating that there is more than one in the Godhead] to know good and evil: Therefore the Lord sent him forth from the Garden of Eden, to till the ground from whence he was taken. So he drove out the man" (Gen: 4:22-24). We know that Eve was with her husband when they were driven out; however, she is not mentioned because God only saw one person, Adam. Likewise, God declared, "Hear O Israel the Lord thy God is one God," (Mark 12:29). There is no division in God. Our Lord Jesus by the shedding of his blood and the Spirit of adoption we receive from God has made us part of the Holy family: "For we are members of his body, of his flesh, and of his bones," reads the scripture: 'For this cause shall a man leave his father and mother, and be joined to his wife, and the two shall be one flesh.' This is a great mystery: but I speak concerning Christ and the Church" (Eph.5:29). What is that mystery? We are connected to God through Jesus, not only in Spirit (for he that is joined to the Lord is one Spirit), but we also make up the physical body of Christ here on earth. On earth we have two different groups of people joining together to form one new man. Those joined to the body have this in common, "The spirit, the water and the blood and these three agree in one, (1John 5:8), or one faith, one baptism and one spirit.

The human body is formed by many cells and every cell, organ, bone, and tissues has its respective functions, so likewise does Jesus and the Church are body with members in all nations. The first Adam who was created out of the dust of the earth, physically manifested the spiritual image and likeness of God. The new Adam was created male and female in the image and likeness of God. "For there are three that bear record in heaven, the Father, the Word and the Holy Ghost, and these three are one. These three bear record in heaven as one family" (John 5:7) God is one like we are one with Christ. This is a revelation I received concerning the holy family in heaven. In a dream I was told that the name Jesus represents the corporate power of the triune God in heaven. These three operate as one. They are separate but not equal. Jesus testified that his Father is greater than all (John 10:29).

Another example of the holy family is found in the birth of Jesus. Mary was told by the angel Gabriel, "The Holy Ghost shall come upon thee and the power of the highest shall overshadow thee: therefore that holy thing that shall be born of thee shall be called the Son of God" (Lu.1:35). Mary was the first recorded surrogate mother in human history. Truly the wisdom of this world is foolishness with God. God was responsible for the virgin birth phenomenon two thousand years ago, and medical science today presents it as though it is something new. There is nothing new under the sun. Biogenetic engineering and gene manipulation are not new. From the DNA strands of David, God created a body in which they placed the Spirit of their Son. This they implanted into a womb and brought forth a Savior. He was a man in every respect because he was the son of man. Yet he was God in every respect because he was the Son of God and thus equal to God and declared to be God by his Father (Heb.1:3-10).

CHAPTER THREE

Darkness Separated from Light

The goal of this chapter is to establish death as a spiritual being that rules over the kingdom of darkness. This being was coequal with the first light and was called Night. This we know from the scriptures. For after the Spirit of God moved upon the face of the waters that covered the deep darkness, "God said let there be light. And God saw the light that it was good and God divided the light from the darkness. And the light he called Day, and the darkness He called Night. And the evening and the morning were the first day (Gen1:1-5).

That was the beginning of the separation of two groups of spirits. One group was called evil and lived on the earth and below the earth. They were confined to the darkness as their natural habitat. The works of these were called "evil." The other group was called "good" and lived in heaven and also on the earth. These two groups each had a leader to rule over them. In the book of Revelation, we read that Jesus is the beginning of the creation of God, the first light, which was separated from the darkness and given to rule over the children of light or the day (John 1:4-5). Death was also given a kingdom and spirits to rule over. Just as the blackness of night is different from a bright, sunny day, so Death is different from his opposite life, but they are both knowledgeable about the things of God. God placed the two in his special garden where he also placed man, the last of his creation.

Death Enters the World

How Death entered the world is a question that I believe we all ask ourselves at some point as we journey through earth. We know that it is appointed unto man once to die, then after that, face the judgment. We all have lost a friend, a loved one, or in one form or the other, witnessed death. It all began with our first parents, Adam and Eve,

God's perfect creation. They were told by God to avoid the tree of the knowledge of good and evil, which was in the center of the Garden of Eden. I want the reader to understand that by partaking of its fruits, man exposed himself to a host of undesirable and harmful spirits. Death used Satan's cunning and wisdom to deceive man and bring him into subjection. Man, by his very nature, was supposed to rule over the spirits, but not be in subjection to them. By submitting to the trickery of the serpent, man gave death, power over him. That was not, and is still not, a natural process. Man was created to live, and not die. When Death entered the world through man's sinful act of disobedience, it brought with it the evils of sickness, disease, pain, and suffering of the flesh and the mind.

Death also brought about a separation of man from God's Holy Spirit (Titus 3:5). When death first entered Adam, it corrupted his mind, filling him with evil thoughts. Man became preoccupied with lies and materialistic and wicked desires. The desire for sin begins with the inner man or the spirit. For out of the heart (spirit) proceeds evil thoughts, murders, adulteries, fornications, thefts, false witness, and blasphemies. These are the things that defile a man. The fruits of God's divine spiritual laws, which gave man light, were no longer governing the mind of Adam after he sinned.

The Conflict in the Flesh

When the spirit of Death entered the flesh, another spirit occupied man's temple, which was created for God's Holy Spirit. Death brought in by the spirit of sin, which led man to his physical demise. That spirit of the world was passed unto all man. That is why all have sinned. Not because of a physical act, but because of the spiritual occupation of sin. The apostle, Paul, clearly wrote about the conflict that man endures because of sin. He wrote, "But I see another law in my members, warring against the law of my mind, and bringing me into captivity of the law of sin which is in my members. O wretched man that I am! Who shall deliver me from the body of this death?" (Rom 7: 23-24) To avoid spiritual death, one must walk in obedience to the law of God, to see Death, practice sin. That process of how death works and how to overcome its effect is neatly summed up in the book of Ephesians. "And you had he quicken who were dead in trespasses and sins. Wherein in time past you walked according to the coast of this world the spirit that now worketh in the children of disobedience: Among whom we all had our conversation in time past in the lust of the flesh, fulfilling the desires of the flesh and of the mind; and were by nature the children of wrath even as others. But God, who is rich in mercy, for his great love wherewith he loved us, even when we were dead in sins, hath quickened us together with Christ. (by grace are ye saved) (Eph 2:1-5). We can be alive through obedience or dead because of disobedience. The spirit is made alive through the operation of God, who through the grace of his Holy Spirit renews a spiritual relationship with our spirit. You must be born again of water and of Spirit.

Where Do We Go from Here?

At the time of physical death, the spirit that occupies the body created from dust, leaves the body to go and live with its master in the kingdom of death. (Physical death begins not with the cessation of vital organs, but with the separation of spirit from the body [James 2:26].) The experience of facing death and going to that land where death awaits man's spirit was described by Job who said, "Before I go whence I shall not return, even to the land of darkness and the shadow of death; a land of darkness itself; and of the shadow of death, without any order, and where light is as darkness" (Job 12: 21). That place was once "the house appointed for all living" (Job 30:26). From the land of darkness the place of Death's throne and his kingdom, death feeds on the soul of those who die without Jesus as Lord of their lives; while the worms eat their flesh in the grave (see Psalms 49:14).

Satan tempts man and lures him to sin. Man sins and becomes a servant to that spirit which leads him to death. When a person dies outside of Christ, they become a prisoner of death. They are kept in a place called hell. In hell, their sins and iniquities that were not forgiven, become the weight that holds them in hell. It is as if a man was convicted and sentenced to prison to serve life. The freedom to go and visit or to have peace and quiet rest is taken away. Think of a place where chaos reigns and around you are the worst sort of evil, wicked people. That is what is waiting those who choose to be with Death. Death is a cruel lord and has no mercy or compassion, but "love is strong as death" (Song Sol. 8:6). God so loved us that He sent love into the world to rescue us from Death. "For we must all die, and are as water spilt on the ground, which cannot be gathered up again; neither doth God respect any person; yet doth he devise means, that his banished be not expelled from him (2 Sam. 14:14).

Victory over Death

We can escape spiritual banishment from God and have life in the first resurrection by believing and trusting in Jesus. For Jesus declared, "I Am the resurrection, and the life: he that believeth in me, though he were dead, yet shall he live: and whosoever liveth and believeth in me shall never die. Believest thou this?" We do not see death because we go to be with the Lord in a better place to wait for the resurrection. As born again, blood washed, Holy Ghost-filled believers, we no longer need to fear death. Death and the grave have no power over us who believe Jesus is the Son of God. Jesus gave us hope when he said, "Verily, verily I say unto you, He that heareth my words, and believest on him that sent me, hath everlasting life, and shall not come into condemnation; but is passed from death unto life. Verily, verily I say unto you, the hour is coming, and now is, when the dead shall hear the voice of the son of God: and they that hear shall live" (John 5:24-25).

Paul and Peter, the apostles, also wrote that when they put off the body of this house, that they look forward to their new house and to be with the Lord. Paul said he had rather be with the Lord than to be here on earth. So believers need not worry about death, for they go to a place of light, and not to the land of darkness.

The New Man

On that day when our corrupted bodies, are changed to those that are incorruptible, and our mortality is changed to immortality, we can boldly say, "O death, where is your sting, O Hades [grave] where is your victory? The sting of death is sin, and the strength of sin is the law. But thanks be to God who gives us the victory through our Lord Jesus Christ" (1 Cor.15:55-57). God also said through the prophet Hosea, "I will redeem them from the power of the grave; I will redeem them from death: O death, I will be thy plagues; O grave I will be thy destruction: repentance shall be hid from my eyes" (Hosea 13:14). Even Death, the last enemy, will be subjected to God. "At the name of Jesus, every knee will bow, and every tongue will confess that Jesus Christ is Lord to the glory of God the Father, whether it be things on earth, or things in heaven, or things under the earth, which includes Death" (Phil. 2:10).

The Armies of Death

The spiritual forces that were first associated with Death are not to be confused with the devil and his angels who originally were part of the kingdom of light. When those angels who first sinned were cast down into darkness, they became the devils that that are associated with different sickness and behaviors who torment men upon earth and probably under the earth. The spirits associated with Death are the deadly and harmful bacteria and diseases found in the earth, as well as spirits who live under the earth.

Evil spirits existed in the darkness, when God separated the spirits of light from those of darkness that were living in their own allotted space. So along with Death, there exists an army of angels or spirits that is responsible for all of the evil in the world. These spirits influence governments, empires, and universal forces.

Who Governs the World?

The knowledge of evil was released into men through man's disobedience, and Death came with sin. The sting of sin is Death. The body of evil and deadly spirits is controlled by Death. These work in harmony with other evil angels whose place is still in heaven. "We wrestle not with flesh and blood, but against principalities and powers, against the rulers of darkness of this world, against spiritual wickedness in high places" (Eph.6:12). They operate in the highest levels of government; they formulate the laws and set the educational standards. They are the root cause of evil that roams the earth and the heavens. Death will rule over them in the grave as Satan lures them to destruction. These triads of evil whose roots are deeply embedded in darkness have combined forces to fight against God. The enemies of God—Death, and Satan, and Hell, have combined forces to destroy the people and the works of God. Through pseudo science, false religion, and spiritual deception, they deceive people into trusting in man rather than in God. They twist the truth of things in nature and the scriptures, to promote falsehood. To those who do not know the depths of Satan as they speak, nor hold to the doctrine of Jezebel, Jesus promised to give power over the nations (Rev. 2:19-24).

CHAPTER FOUR

Spirits Have no Flesh or Bones

First of all, Jesus said that a spirit does not have flesh and bones (Lu.24:39). His disciples saw him crucified and died on the cross, so when he appeared before them, they thought they saw a spirit. Every living creature has a spirit or spirits living in them, but every spirit does not have a body to live in. It is possible to see and converse with spirits, just as it is possible to see and converse with angels. A good example of the discussion as to the existence of spirits is found in the Book of Acts. There was an ongoing dispute between the Sadducees and the Pharisees. The Sadducees said that there is not any resurrection, neither angel nor spirit, but the Pharisees confessed them both. They believed that a spirit or an angel hath spoken to Paul, who said he had seen the resurrected Lord Jesus. They believed that spirits can be heard and seen, but that they are different from angels who have flesh and bones.

Different Spiritual Life Forms

There are different types of life forms in heaven that I want to mention that has a spirit living in them, or are spirits. Let us look first at angels. Angels are described by the Psalmist as spirits "Who maketh his angels spirits." However, throughout the Bible, we read about angels interacting with humans. We are warned to entertain strangers because we just might be entertaining an angel. So we can safely say that some angels look like humans. The angels were created with greater strength and wisdom than man. The Psalmist points that out when he asked the question: "What is man that thou art mindful of him? And the son of man that thou visitest him? For thou hast made him a little lower than the angels" (Psalm 8:4-5). The apostle, Peter, reaffirmed that in 2 Peter 2:11 while comparing man to them. He said, "Whereas angels who are greater in power and might," indicating both physical and spiritual superior strengths of our celestial counterparts. These created beings were given bodies that are different than that which was given to man.

Duties of Angels

The angels from their respective locales are assigned their specific duties, one of which is to protect and deliver the saints. One of their jobs is protecting man, whom they call their brothers, from danger and evil influences. "The angels of the Lord encamp round about them that fear him to deliver them" (Psalms 34:7). God said to Israel, "Behold I send an angel before thee, to keep thee in the way, and to bring thee into the place which I have prepared. Beware of him, and obey his voice, provoke him not; for he will not pardon your transgressions: for my name is in him. But if thou shalt obey his voice, and do all that I speak; then I will be an enemy to thine enemies, and an adversary unto thine adversaries. For mine angel shall go before thee, and bring thee in unto the land of [the list of nations] . . . And I will cut them off" (Ex 23:20-23). This is a special angel who bore the name of the Lord and had authority to correct the children of Israel as he led them into the land of promise. We can safely call him a body guard or the front guard and captain of the people in the wilderness. The angel met Joshua before the Battle of Jericho with his sword drawn. When Joshua saw him, he asked him if he was for Israel or against Israel. The angel's reply was to identify himself as the captain of the host of the Lord (Joshua 5: 14). Throughout the reading of the Old and New Testament, we find an ongoing relationship between God, man, and angels. The angels were sent by God to guide us, fight along side of us, or to punish us as we read in the book of Chronicles. "And god sent an angel unto Jerusalem to destroy it: and as he was destroying the Lord beheld, and he repented him of the evil, and said to the angel that destroyed, 'It is enough, stay now thine hand'" (1 Chron. 20:15).

When Peter was in jail and about to be beheaded, God sent an angel to free him from prison (Acts 12:7-8). God also sent an angel to speak to Cornelius, the devout Gentile. God still send angels to speak to us, and they are still active in the lives and the affairs of this generation.

Angels at War

Some angels are assigned to bring messages from God to mankind. Some angels fight against evil angels that seek to discourage or harm humans. The same way nations have strife and war against each other on earth, so also the celestial planet is plagued with strife and war. A good example of these activities in the celestial realm, and the effects they have on earth, is found in the book of Daniel. Daniel was praying and fasting in hope of receiving a revelation from God. The Angel Gabriel was sent to bring the revelation to him. However, for two weeks, Gabriel was held up by an opposing angel who was the prince of Persia. For two weeks, they fought until Michael came (one of the chief angels) and helped Gabriel so that he could get through to Daniel with the message (Dan. 10:13). After Gabriel delivered the message to Daniel, he returned and continued to fight with the prince of Persia. "The prince of the kingdom of Persia withstood me one and twenty days but lo, Michael, one of the chief princes came to help me . . . and now will I return to fight with the prince of Persia and when I am gone forth, lo the prince of Grecia shall come" (Dan. 10:13, 20). When one kingdom ruler goes, another one rises up in his place. Notice how Gabriel was fighting with the Prince of Persia, and afterward, the prince of Greece was to come forth.

Daniel, at the time of this visitation by the Angel Gabriel, was an officer in the kingdom of Cyrus, King of Persia. After Persia fell, the Greek Empire began according to the word of the angel. The invisible rulers are very much responsible for what takes place in the visible earth: "For we wrestle not against flesh and blood, but against principalities, against powers, against the rulers of the darkness of this world, against spiritual wickedness in high places" (Eph. 6:12).

The Heavens Rule

Angels and spirits influence governments, people, direct wars, and generate the policies that govern societies. Every man is influenced by some spirit that plays upon his fleshly appetite for pleasure and power. Angels are engaged daily in causing this one to survive and allowing that one to meet a destructive end. Every celestial body, moon, stars, sun, and the surrounding planets influence each other. These are all interdependent. Likewise, human and angels, and other celestial beings influence each other in some way, and we are all interdependent.

King Nebuchadnezzar understood the powerful influence from heaven after he was dethroned and lived like a wild animal for seven years. His judgment came from heaven. "This matter is by the decree of the watchers, and the demand by the work of the holy ones: to the intent that the living may know that the Most High ruleth in the kingdom of men and giveth to whomsoever he will and setteth up over it the bases of man" (Dan. 4:17). The King was driven from his kingdom by forces greater than himself and powers that the kingdom of Babylon could not stand up against.

After the Lord had humbled King Nebuchadnezzar, the humbled king praised the God of Heaven saying, "I Bless the Most High and I praise and honor him that lived forever, whose dominion is an everlasting dominion and his kingdom is from generation to generation; and all inhabitants of the earth are reputed as nothing and he doeth according to his will in the army of heaven and among the inhabitants of the earth, and none can stay his hand and say unto him what does thou . . . now I Nebuchadnezzar praise and extol and honor the King of Heaven, all whose works are true and his ways judgment; and those who walk in pride he is able to abase" (Dan. 4-35:37). He understood that God breaks in pieces, mighty men, without number. It is God who sets them up, and when they get too proud or arrogant, is able to sit them down.

Spirits and the Fulfillment of Prophecy

God, as we read, rules over the armies of heaven who help in the governing of the affairs of man on earth. The role of the spiritual influence is what makes the fulfillment of prophecy so certain. The prophet Isaiah reiterated that fact when he wrote that God's "word will not return to him without accomplishing the thing he pleases, or prospering in the thing he sent it to." God is the director, the author, and finisher of our faith. Through the networking of angels and other invisible creatures, spirit life directly impacts our behavior and thoughts. In the Lord's Prayer, Jesus prayed, "Thy will be done on earth as it is in heaven." He also said to his disciples, "Whatsoever you bind on earth I will bind in heaven, and whatsoever you lose on earth I will lose in heaven." Those are powerful indicators of the impact that the life from heaven has on the life on earth.

The Roles of Angels

We read of the angels and their varied role in fulfilling prophesies from the book of Revelation. We read of the angel who is responsible to offer up the prayers of the saints before God: "And another angel came and stood at the altar, having a golden censer, and there was given unto him much incense, that he should offer it with the prayers of all saints upon the altar which was before the throne."

We can also read about the angel who opened the bottomless pit. When he opened it, the scripture says, "And there arose a smoke out of the pit, as the smoke of a great furnace; and the sun and the air were darkened by reason of the smoke of the pit."

From out of the pit, there came an angel who was in charge of those horrible creatures that will ascend out of the pit: "And they had a king over them, which is the angel of the bottomless pit, whose name in the Hebrew tongue is Abaddon, but in the Greek tongue hath his name, Apollyon" (Rev.9:1-2, 11).

Angels are also responsible for the wind: "And after these things I saw four angels standing on the for four corners of the earth, holding the four winds of the earth, that the wind should not blow on the earth, nor the sea, nor on any tree." Yet another angel is responsible for sealing the servants of God in their foreheads: "And I saw another angel ascending from the east, having the seal of the living God: and he cried with a loud voice to the four angels, to whom it was given to hurt the earth and the sea, saying, 'Hurt not the earth, neither the sea, nor the trees, till we have sealed the servants of our God in their foreheads'" (Rev 7:1-2). There is an angel who is over the water (Rev16:5) and an angel who has power over fire (Rev 14:18).

There is an angel who will dry up the rivers, and there are angels who fight in heaven and earth. There are angels responsible for opening seals, and sending plagues unto the earth, and fulfilling the word of prophecy and the counsel of God (Rev.15:1). When you are born again into the family of God and are part of His kingdom, all those angels work on your behalf. You need not fear the angels of Death, Hell, and Satan who are part of the kingdom of darkness. I want the readers to picture in their minds the activities of angels and their vital role in the affairs of God and man. They traverse the heavens and the earth executing the will of God and fulfilling his word.

Holy Angels Reverence God

Another feature about angels is that the holy ones do not desire to be worshiped by man. The angel forbid John worshipping him saying, "See thou do it not: for I am thy fellow servant, and of thy brethren the prophets, and of them which keep the commandments of God: Worship God" (Rev. 22:9). So we do have angels that consider us their kin, and they serve us in the fight against the enemies of God. When we learn to connect to the resources from heaven, we will understand what it means to have friends and family in high places.

Angels are sent forth to minister to man and were commanded from the beginning to worship the Son of God. "When he bringeth the first born into the world, he saith, and let all the angels of God worship him." These all serve the Lord Jesus and worship him and the God of heaven, just like we humans do. The Psalmist said that the chariots of God number "twenty thousands even thousands of angels." "The Lord is among them as in Sinai, in the holy place." Angels were given the job of protecting man from danger and evil influences. "The angels of the Lord encamp round about them that fear him to deliver them" (Psalms 34:7).

Angels Have Different Types of Celestial Bodies

Angels are spirits who live in a body given to them by God. It is possible for them to lose that body, just as it is possible for man to die and lose his body. There are also evil angels and evil spirits who do the will of God. We will read more about the evil ones in another section. I want to mention the good ones in this section. Along with angels, there are other creatures that make up the celestial host in the kingdom of God.

In the book of Isaiah, we read about the heavenly creatures he called the Seraphims. These he described as having six wings. "With twain he covered his face, and with twain he covered his feet, and with twain he did fly" (Isa.6:2). The commercially designed angel that we see, looks nothing like the Seraphims. We usually see the commercial ones having a set of wings. Do they actually look like those images we see? From the angels I had the privilege of seeing, I never saw wings. That does not mean that some angels don't have wings—I did not see any on those angels the Lord allowed me to see.

However, in the book of Zechariah, we read of two women who have wings. "Then I lifted up mine eyes, and looked, and, behold, there came out two women, and the wind was in their wings; for they had wings of a stork: and they lifted up the ephah between the earth and the heaven" (Zech 5:9). Who are those women, are they angels or just another group of celestial creatures?

Angels Who Transport God

The prophet Ezekiel describes another set of creatures with wings that he called Cherubims. In a vision, he saw God riding the Cherubim whom he called the living creatures. He described the four of them that he saw as follows: "And this was their appearance; they had the likeness of a man. And every one had four faces, and every one had four wings. And their feet were straight feet; and the sole of their feet was like the sole of a calf's foot: and they sparkled like the color of burnished brass." The reader should pay attention to their feet that are like the sole of a calf's foot. These are called the living creatures because they exhibit features of both man and beast. Yet they are continually in the presence of God, crying, "Holy holy is the Lord" (Rev. 4:8).

The difference between the Cherubims and the Seraphims is that the Cherubims have four wings, while the Seraphims have six.

The prophet further described them as having hands under their wings on their four sides. Their wings were joined, and they moved as one unit. Their faces were of four different creatures: a man, a lion, an ox, and an eagle, all on one body. These looked like burning coals of fire, with flashes of fire that looked liked flashes of lightning coming out of them. The creatures themselves moved with the speed of lightning.

These creatures had another distinguishing feature, a wheel. "The appearance of the wheels and their works were alike unto the colour of a beryl: and they four had one likeness: and their appearance and their work, was as it were, a wheel in the middle of a wheel." Talk about a set of wheels, wow! I don't know of anyone on earth who can boast about riding such a magnificent creature. The wheels went wherever the living creatures went because the spirit of the living creatures was in the wheels. The spirit of the living creatures is in the wheels just as the spirit of man is in his body. The wheel responded to the spirit just as our bodies respond to the will of our spirit.

Picture this scene," And there appeared in the Cherubim the form of a man's hand under their wings . . . And their whole body, and their backs, and their hands, and their wings, and the wheels, were full of eyes round about, even the wheels that they four had." The wheels that housed the spirits of the living creatures had some distinguishing features of their own. The wheels also had four faces: "the first face was the face of a Cherub, and the second face was the face of a man, and the third the face of a lion, and the fourth the face of an eagle" (Ezekiel 1:10). Like the living creatures that Isaiah saw whose body was unique to them, so also the Cherubims are unique and have that special role of transporting God through the heavens. I don't think any man would ever be able to compare his means of transportation with that of God.

The lord showed me in a dream two of the living creatures. They stood upright because their chest and legs appeared to be that of a man. However, from their shoulders upward, they were different from anything that I have ever seen. One of the faces that I saw looked like an eagle or hawk. I could not differentiate clearly between what type of bird it was. From the neck up it had feathers which were a combination of different shades of browns with very little black lines towards the end. The wings were very wide, wide enough to cover parts of the body. As I was watching the creature in the dream as it passed by me, I saw a head extended above the wings that looked like a human head. It had no hair, and the color was light blue like that of a blue and white cloud mixed together. There were no noticeable eyebrows, and the eyes were round. It extended its hand to give me something, and the hand was covered with feathers like the feathers on a bird legs. Did the creature have two heads or was one of the heads on the other creature whose head I did not see when I initially saw the creatures. Their face was covered and I saw the head from the side as they passed me with one of the wings covering the bird head and most of the body.

Spirits of Fire

Another body of spirits are those that appear as flames of fire. The flames of fire are spirits from God that minister through humans. John the Baptist made mention of baptism by fire when he told his followers, "I indeed baptize you with water unto repentance: but he that cometh after me is mightier than I, whose shoes I am not worthy to bear: he shall baptize you with the Holy Ghost and with fire" (Mat. 3:11).

The Jews, before Jesus came into the world to die for our sins, also had spiritual experiences and dealt with different kinds of spirits. However, after Jesus came into the world, the Jews had another spiritual experience. John the Baptist mentions two different baptisms to the Jews who came to be baptized by him. John said to the people who came: "I indeed baptize you with water; but one mightier than I cometh, the latchet of whose shoes I am not worthy to unloose: he shall baptize you with the Holy Ghost and with fire" Lu 3:16. John mentioned two baptism that by the Holy Ghost, and the fire. The fire and the Holy Ghost baptism by the apostles on the day of Pentecost are two distinct manifestations. First, the rushing wind came and filled the house. So there was a presence of the Spirit. Then there was a manifestation of fire. "And there appeared unto them cloven tongues like of fire, and it sat upon each of them. And they were all filled with the Holy Ghost, and began to speak with other tongues as the Spirit gave them utterance" (Acts2:3-4). The apostles received the fullness from two spiritual entities: the Father and the Mother. The Spirits of the Father are the manifestation of fire.

Another example of spirits as fire is found in the book of Kings. Elisha the prophet was surrounded by the Syrian army. The young man who served him saw the soldiers of the Syrian army and asked, "How shall we do?" Elijah's response was to pray that God would open the young man's eyes that he may see. "And the Lord opened the eyes of the young man; and he saw: and behold, the mountain was full of horses and chariots of fire round about Elisha." The chariots were made of fire, and who was in the chariots?

Moses was met in the wilderness by the angel in the burning bush when he was called by God. After he led the children of Israel out of Egypt and he went up the Sinai Mountain to receive the commandments and to talk with God, the mountain was on fire. God dwells in the midst of the flame. "For our God is a consuming fire," said the Hebrew writer (Heb 12:29).

Qualities of the Father

The Spirit that came upon Moses and the kings of Israel not only fought for them, but also stood side by side with them in every situation of their life. Therefore, Moses and the children of Israel called God a man of war (Ex. 15:3). That Spirit of God that was with Moses brought great calamities upon the enemies of Israel and instilled fear in them. Some of that same Spirit that was upon Moses, was also upon the seventy elders. Together they shared in the raising up of the nation of Israel. It was always the Spirit that was manifested to them and to their enemies. That same Spirit that was with Moses was also with Joshua, who destroyed nations through war as he led the children into the Promised Land. The Spirit of God left King Saul and rested upon King David, and David was known as a man of war. That was the Father, the one engulfed in the flame. "Our God is a consuming fire" (Heb 12:29). The scriptures are filled with examples of the fire of God and how God fights for those who trust and obey Him, that is not the same Spirit of promise that the Christians receive when baptized in the Holy Ghost.

Baptism in the Holy Ghost

The born again, Spirit filled Christians, receive the Holy Ghost, or that other Spirit that Jesus spoke to his disciples about. One day the disciples wanted to call down fire from heaven to destroy a city that did not receive Jesus. Jesus rebuked them and said to them, "Ye know not of what spirit you are of." In other words this other Spirit is here to save and to heal all manner of sickness and diseases, and to cast out devils, and to do cures, and to bring salvation and peace on earth and good will to all man. The Holy Ghost teaches forgiveness and compassion and how to show love to our neighbors not grudgingly, but from a pure heart. This is the nature of the Spirit of Jehovah, the Mother who had never left the side of her beloved Son. The visible picture we were left with was that of Mary who was at her Son's side even to his hour of death on Calvary cross.

Jesus promised his disciples power after the Holy Ghost came upon them (Acts 1:8). This legal occupation by the Holy Ghost manifests the gifts of the Spirit, as well as the fruit of the Spirit, in the lives of the believers. This is the promise of the Father which is reserved in heaven waiting to be given to everyone that asks. These spiritual entities have no physical or material form, but inhabit the human body enabling us to not only communicate with God, but to also demonstrate the power of God.

Some Qualities of the Holy Ghost

The Lord showed me in a vision a cloud of doves, each one individually separated from the other, but they were so close to each other that they looked like one body that formed into a cloud in the sky. In another vision I saw them sent down upon the earth like pouring rain in the forms of gifts to be received by men. When those filled with these Spirits are gathered together in one place, the manifestation of the divine power is present to do miracles and all the works of God because the spiritual gifts are granted with the Spirit we receive from heaven. This power resides in the church of the living God and enables the saints of God to have power over spirits, disease and all the power of the enemy.

After Jesus sent out his seventy disciples, they returned with the report, "Lord even the devils are subject unto us through thy name." His response was;" I beheld Satan as lightning fall from heaven. Behold I give you power to tread on serpents and scorpions, and over all the power of the enemy and nothing shall by any means hurt you. Notwithstanding, in this rejoice not that the spirits are subject to you, but rather rejoice because your name is written in heaven" Lk 10:18-20. Through the power of the Holy Ghost, man is able to unlock the mysteries of the kingdom of God and was granted authority over spirits to bind and to lose them. Jesus, before his final ascension into heaven, told his disciples to wait for the promise of the Father and that they would receive power after the Holy Ghost came upon them. He fulfilled the scripture, "When he ascended on high he led captivity captive and gave gifts unto men" (Eph. 4:8). The gift being the Holy Ghost with whom God seals the believers and through whom they are sanctified. "Now there are diversities of gifts, but the same Spirit," (1Cor. 12:4) that operates as one within the bodies of those appointed by God. As the Spirit is one, the body of believers is united through the Spirit working in them.

After the transgression in the Garden of Eden, man was separated from the Holy Ghost and the living Word and could no longer live forever. "But after that the kindness and the love of God, our Savior, toward man, appeared not by works of righteousness which we have done, but according to his mercy he saved us, by the washing of regeneration, and renewing of the Holy Ghost; which he shed on us abundantly through Jesus Christ our Savior; that being justified by his grace, we should be heirs according to the hope of eternal life" (Titus 3:4-7). The restoration began with Jesus, the living word, who promised out of our bellies shall flow rivers of living water. The living water is the Holy Ghost which they that believe Jesus receive. (John 7:38-39).

Conclusion

The baptism with the Holy Ghost and Fire, the anointing of the Spirit of God upon a person's life to perform miracles, healings, wonder, and great signs from heaven through the power and Spirit of God is reserved for the faithful who are called to glory. This generation will see the awesome power of God as is told by the prophets, as prophecy unfolds before their eyes. Through faith we are able to receive God Spirit and the assistance from angels who serve God. Every believer should seek to be baptized in the Spirit. For, "If any man has not the spirit of Christ, he is none of his. But if the Spirit of him that raised up Jesus from the dead dwell in you, he that rose up Jesus from the dead shall also quicken your mortal bodies by his Spirit that dwelleth in you" (Rom 8:9, 11

CHAPTER FIVE

The Many Faces of Satan

To write about Satan is to write about another one of the great mysteries of the Bible. Much is written about Satan who is also called the Old Serpent, the Great Red Dragon, and the Devil (Rev.12:9) in the Bible. In this chapter, I hope to show that each of those names represents a symbolic personality of this created being. As we interpret the symbolic language used to describe this angelic majesty, I hope to show the prophetic role that will be fulfilled by this entity.

The Devil is called by different names for a reason. Each name represents a personality or a manifestation of him: the Serpent deceived Eve; the Devil tempted Jesus in the wilderness and declared himself to be the ruler of the kingdoms of the world; Satan entered into Judas and led him to the murderers of Jesus our Lord; and the Dragon is manifested as the physical image of the kingdom of Satan after which the kingdoms of the world on earth are patterned.

In the book of Genesis, he is called the serpent that was the most subtle/wisest of all the beasts of the field that God had created (Gen 3:1). Through his wisdom and his brightness, he deceived Eve in the garden to which he had access, and caused her to eat the forbidden fruit. The apostle, Paul, reiterated this by saying, "But I fear, lest by any means, as the serpent beguiled Eve through his subtlety" (2 Cor.11:3), or through his keen insight, and wisdom he was able to deceive Eve. Jesus also spoke of his wisdom when he told his disciples, "Be ye therefore, wise as serpents, and harmless as doves" (Matt.10:16). Jesus mentions serpents, indicating that serpent refers to not just Satan, but to the other spirits and evil angels that follow him.

Satan put it in the hearts of Ananias and Sapphira to lie to the Holy Ghost about a piece of property they bought. Those lies caused them their life (Acts. 5:1-10). Satan also entered into Judas Iscariot, the night he went out to betray the Lord Jesus (John 13:26). It is easy to see the pattern as to how Satan sets people up for destruction. Satan seduces and entices man to sin. In John 13:2, we read that he prompted Judas to betray our Lord. Then when Judas was fully receptive of the temptation, Satan entered him to execute the action.

Satan hindered Paul from going to Thessalonians (1Thes 2:18), and who knows how many other undocumented encounters there are where Satan hindered someone, and they got discouraged and turned away from their blessing. It could have been a man of the cloth or a trusted leader who was under Satan's influence and stopped you. In heaven, he is called the accuser of the brethren, who accuses them before God, day and night. (Rev. 12:10) He walks up and down the earth as a roaring lion seeking whom he may devour or ensnare in an act of rebellion against God. (1 Pet. 5:8). Some people have no clue as to why they do what they do. Yes, sometimes the devil made them do it. Resist the devil and he will flee from you. (Ja. 4:7)

The devil is sometimes used by God to test the faith of man, as we saw with Job. But, as we read in 1 Cor. 5:5, the apostle, Paul, when writing to the church at Corinth in regard to one of the members who had grievously sinned, suggested, "To deliver such a one to Satan for the destruction of the flesh, that the spirit may be saved in the day of the Lord Jesus." (1 Cor. 5:5) God had prepared the wicked for the day of evil and man can use the power of Satan to maintain order in the church of God. The apostle Paul was also buffeted by a messenger of Satan to keep him humble. (2 Cor. 12:7)

From an Angel of Light to the Prince of Darkness

When God made the worlds, Satan was given authority to rule over certain angels and a place to govern. This we learn from the prophet, Ezekiel, who was given revelations about Satan. Man was given the earth to rule and to have dominion over, and Satan and his angels were given a place in heaven to rule. All the leaders of God's creation met in a place called the Garden of Eden, and there they congregated to meet with God.

The prophet saw Satan first as a king (but not the King of Kings) who was given a land that Ezekiel called Tyrus. The prophet wrote, "Son of man, take up a lamentation upon the king of Tyrus, and say unto him, Thus saith the Lord God; 'Thou sealest up the sum full of wisdom, and perfect in beauty.'" (Eze 28:12) The apostle, Jude, described him as an angelic majesty, and cautions us to regard him as such. Jude, in speaking about those who speak evil of dignities, said that Michael, the archangel, when disputing with the devil, dared not bring against him a railing accusation, but said to him, "The Lord rebuke thee" (Jude 9). Even the Lord Jesus said to him, "Get behind me, Satan" and quoted the scriptures when he was tempted by him and referred to him as the prince of this world. Mt 4:, John 14:30, 16:11

Satan and his angels rule from their place in heaven and travel back and forth from heaven to earth. We read about the prince of Persia, an angel operating in the kingdom of Satan, who hindered the angel Gabriel for twenty one days from bringing a message to Daniel. (Dan 10:13) From the book of Job, we learned that Satan reports to the assembly in heaven. At one of those gatherings Satan asked God to allow him to afflict Job and was given permission to do so. (Job 1:). Now I must point out that when I say heaven, that there is more than one heaven that the Bible refers to. Paul said he was caught up to the third heaven (2Cor:12:2). David, in the book of Psalms, wrote about the heaven of heavens, and in the beginning, God created the heavens and the earth (Gen 2:1,4; Psalms 148:4). Where exactly in heaven is Satan located? I do not know.

The Tree and the Serpent: Man's Relationship to Others in the Garden

This revelation I saw in a dream concerning the tree and the system of government it represents. In the dream I saw a tree with its roots reaching down to hell. It looked like the tree was nourished by the darkness of hell or the world below the earth. Above ground, the tree had seven main branches with limbs and leaves proceeding out of them. I understood the tree to represent the kingdoms of the world that feed on devilish doctrines. It also represents the Great Red Dragon who is also known as Satan, as well as the king of Tyrus. To clarify that, first let us look at how trees are represented in the scriptures.

There were two trees represented in the Garden of Eden—one is the Tree of Life, the other the Tree of the Knowledge of Good and Evil. The symbolic language of using trees to describe the most important figures in the scriptures, reveals the wisdom of God. The tree is used to describe people: "God said we are trees," (Psalms 1:3). The tree is also used to describe nations and kingdoms. Jesus used the parable of the mustard seed to illustrate how great a kingdom can grow out of a small seed.

In the writings of Ezekiel, the prophet, the Assyrian and Pharaoh, along with other rulers, were described as trees in Eden. He wrote, "Behold, the Assyrian was a cedar in Lebanon with fair branches, and with a shadowing shroud, and of a high stature; and his top was among the thick boughs. The waters made him great, the deep set him up on high with her rivers running round about his plants, and sent out her little rivers unto all the trees of the field." Different kingdoms were represented in the Garden of Eden as trees. The Tree of the Knowledge of Good and Evil and its deep and darkness secret was also in the Garden. Man was to keep away from that tree inhabited by those spirits and the knowledge they possessed.

Ezekiel wrote: "The cedars in the garden of God could not hide him: the fir trees were not like his boughs, and the chestnut trees were not like his branches; nor any tree in the garden of God was like unto him in beauty. I have made him fair by the multitude of his branches: so that all the trees of Eden that were in the garden of God envied him" (Ezekiel 31:3-4, 8-9). What are some of the features of this tree that are similar to the king of Tyrus and the tree Eve lusted after? The tree was full of wisdom and beauty and anointed by God, so it stood out. Eve said the tree was pleasing to the eyes and a tree to be desired to make one wise (Gen 3:6). Both were very attractive and smart.

The Assyrian was also called the serpent by the prophet Isaiah who wrote, "The Lord of Host hath sworn, saying, surely as I have thought, so shall it come to pass; and as I have purposed, so shall it stand: that I will break the Assyrian in my land, and upon my mountain tread him under foot: ten shall his yoke depart from off their shoulders. This is the purposed upon the whole earth: and this is the hand that is stretched out upon all the nations . . . Rejoice not whole Palestine because the rod of him that smote thee is broken; for out of the serpent's root shall come forth a cockatrice, and his fruit shall be a fiery flying serpent" (Isa. 14:24-29).

The old serpent, that deceived Eve, is also called the Devil, and the Dragon. This name Dragon refers to a union of nations and kingdoms in heaven and earth. I want the reader to see the relationships of symbols and how they are connected, in order to paint a clear picture of spirits and their roles in the fulfillment of prophecy. Knowing what we are facing in the invisible realm, and how they are manifested in the natural helps us prepare to effectively fight against them.

The Darkness Manifest on Earth

The kingdom referred to as the Assyrian in the Garden of God and as Leviathan, the crooked serpent, by the prophet Isaiah, is also symbolic of Satan, the old Serpent called the Dragon. Those names refer to the spiritual occupation of worldly governments, religious bodies, and other unholy alliances whose spiritual influences make up the body of spiritual wickedness in high places and are worked out on earth through the institutions that serve them. Nourished from their roots in the pit of hell we see nations arise with evil ambitions to destroy the works and the people of God. John saw this spiritual parallel from heaven and its reflection on earth. He wrote, "And there appeared another wonder in heaven; and behold a great red dragon, having seven heads and ten horns, and seven crowns upon his head. And his tail drew the third part of the stars of heaven, and did cast them to the earth." Rev 12:3

Then he described a beast on earth with the mirror image of the Dragon he saw in heaven. The apostle John wrote, "And I stood upon the sand of the sea, and saw a beast rise up out of the sea, having seven heads and ten horns, and upon his horns seven crowns, and upon his heads the name of blasphemy. And he opened his mouth and in blasphemy against God, to blaspheme his name and his tabernacle, and them that dwell in heaven . . . And the dragon gave him his seat and his power and great authority" (Rev 13:1-2, 6). Satan gives the kingdom of the world to whomsoever he pleases. He told Jesus during the hour of temptation that all the kingdoms of the world were delivered into his hands, and he can give it to whomsoever he pleases (Lk 4:6). The beast that John saw is the fiery flying serpent that will come out of Assyria, who when he arises will want to be like the Most High. Satan and his seed all want to be exalted to heaven. They all lust for power and control. Like their father, they are great traffickers in death and desire to be wealthy. These are the people and governments that control economies. They can shut down and stop the flow of trade because they are in control, as Ezekiel wrote concerning the economic state of the prince of darkness: "O thou that art situate at the entry of the sea, which art a merchant of the people for many isles, Thus said the Lord God; O Tyrus, thou hast said, I am of perfect beauty" (Ezk 27:3). Likewise, the world economies and military power are ruthlessly administered by the most brutish of men, whose god is their belly and who are only interested in material things. They buy human souls and oppress and rob the weak and the poor. They are cruel and show no mercy, yet they appear to prosper. These are inhabited by evil spirits that fill man with lustful, proud, and other evil desires that are manifest in the flesh, as the works of the flesh, mentioned in the book of Galatians, chapter 5, verses 19 to 21.

Satan, as a ruler, works with the forces of Death and Hell, to draw Adam into bondage through lies and the fear of death so as to lead him and his posterity to death and hell. The Devil's desire to have no one greater than him drove him not only to plot against the creation of God, but to conspire with Death and Hell. His ministers teach everything that he knows would be displeasing to God to permanently lock man and his posterity into bondage. To accomplish their wicked plans, Satan, along with Death and Hell, formulated doctrines and rituals that enable man to operate on earth as their ministers. Those that govern in his kingdom on earth are in league with Death, and with Hell are they in agreement as the prophet, Isaiah, pointed out in his prophecy to the rulers of Jerusalem, "Because ye have said, We have made a covenant with death, and with hell are we at agreement; when the overflowing scourge shall pass through, it shall not come unto us: for we have made lies our refuge and under falsehood have we hid ourselves" (Isa. 28:15). How many worldly governments can we point to and say they are rooted and grounded in the truth?

Satan as a Priest

As a priest, he saw the adoration God received, and he wanted to be worshipped like God. "And no marvel; for Satan himself is transformed into an angel of light." So it is no great thing if his ministers present themselves as ministers of righteousness (2 Cor. 11:14-15). We then ought not to look for him as a hideous, ignorant creature, but rather a deceiver acquainted with the heavens and familiar with authority as we read in Ezekiel. When he was placed in the Garden of Eden, he was an angel of light until iniquity was found in him, and he was overcome by darkness. He was also anointed by God as a priest like Aaron, the high priest of Israel.

By comparing Satan's garment with those of the high priest of Israel, we find another example of how things on earth are patterned after things in heaven. He ministered to God and led the congregation of angels in worship. Ezekiel received that revelation and wrote, "Thou art the anointed cherub [a person with a sweet lovely face, *Webster Dictionary*] that covereth and I have set thee so: Thou were upon the holy mountain of God; thou hast walked up and down in the midst of the stones of fire. Thou was perfect in thy ways from the day that thou was created, till iniquity was found in thee . . . Son of man, take up a lamentation upon the king of Tyrus, and say unto him, thus saith the Lord God. Thou sealest up the sum full of wisdom and perfect in beauty. Thou hast been in Eden the garden of God; every precious stone was thy covering, the sardius, topaz, and the diamond, the beryl, the onyx, and the jasper, the sapphire, the emerald, and the carbuncle, and gold: the workmanship of thy tabrets and thy pipes was prepared in the day that thou was created." Notice that there are some similarities between the ephod and the covering of the king. Each stone on the ephod represented a tribe of Israel, and it was also their birthstone. Likewise, each stone on Tyrus represents a kingdom and a group of people under that ruler's power and spiritual influence. I suppose witchcraft, astrology, stargazers, horoscope and other forms of readings all fall under this influence. Isa. 47:12,13.

Moses was instructed to pattern the tabernacle he made after the pattern in heaven, as we read in the book of Hebrews chapter 9, verse 23. The instructions were also for the priestly garments and responsibilities. Aaron was anointed by God to be a high priest who wore the ephod: "And thou shalt put upon him the holy garments and anoint him, and sanctify him; that he may minister unto me in the priest office" (Ex 40:13). The ephod that was made for Aaron was covered with twelve different precious stones and gold (Ex 39:6-15).

Just as the high priest Aaron was allowed into the holy place to intercede for the people, Satan was allowed into the presence of God where he still goes and accuses the saints, day and night. Satan was anointed to minister, and a group of angels were assigned to assist him, as Aaron's sons and the tribe of Levi were given charge of priesthood.

Man and the Forbidden Tree

The name of the fruit that Eve ate in the Garden was called the knowledge of Good and Evil. Eve saw the fruit as one that able to make her wise and a fruit to be desired. She lusted and yielded to the temptation presented by the Serpent. The information the Serpent presented to Eve was knowledge, of things separating the children of light from the children of darkness. The serpent was sharing information that was to be kept secret from man. The fruits of the other trees in the Garden were to be used for food, but the tree of the knowledge of Good and, Adam and Eve were not supposed to touch much less to eat. There was to be no crossing over from light to darkness because the spirit that was in Adam was of the day, and not of the night. Even though the darkness and the light were separated, their affections were toward man. Satan defected to the darkness and set out to gain man's affection. He was successful in getting Adam to submit to the darkness and to rule over his posterity.

Satan knew that some works would keep man from fellowshipping with God which led to his degeneration. It became easy for evil to rule over the degenerate man no longer protected by God. The spirit that was introduced into the world is, "The lust of the flesh, the lust of the eyes, and the pride of this life, is not of the Father, but is of the world: And the world passeth away and the lust thereof" (John 2:16-17). Eve lusted, and through the sin of covetousness, she brought the spirit of sin into the world, and man became a servant of sin and was rewarded with death (Rom. 5:12).

The apostle James wrote, "Whosoever will be a friend of the world is the enemy of God." (Ja. 4:4) The world represents the Dragon, Death, and Hell, and these are contrary to God. It is filled with spirits of deceit, lust for riches, lust for power, the evils of pride, immoral lust, that lead people to kill, steal, and lie, to attain to material wealth and possession. Through his deceptions, Satan caused the whole world to be out of course, and be filled with wickedness and darkness. Man's cruelty to his fellowman is rooted in the power of evil associated with the forces of darkness that rules this world. Those vices that are found both in the Old and New Testament keep people today away from God and are all forbidden fruits that lead to death. Death and Hell rule their kingdom in the world beneath the earth, in a place called hell. Satan was given power to rule over a kingdom in the heavens, and he has established a kingdom on earth. Together the three represent the spiritual kingdom of light and darkness whose fruits are the knowledge of good and evil.

Pride and Envy, Two Deadly Sins

What motivated Satan to act so treacherously in the Garden of Eden? The prophet Ezekiel sheds some light on that question. He wrote of Satan, "Thine heart was lifted up because of thy beauty; thou hast corrupted thy wisdom by reason of thy brightness." His beauty and his wisdom deceived him. Most of what he told Eve was the truth because he was acquainted with the truth. However, not only was his wisdom corrupted, but we will also learn that the sin of pride precedes destruction as the scripture reads: "Pride goes before destruction and a haughty spirit before a fall" (Prov.16:18).

His role was to minister to man, and to lead the heavenly choir in worship and praise to the Lord. Iniquity was found in him, and he rebelled against God for giving man an exalted position. The angels were to serve man and through Jesus, worship man. Satan wanted to be like the Most High to receive worship and praise. Jealous of God and full of envy, Satan sought to destroy the works of God by introducing lies to turn people away from the truth and believe a lie, and not worship and serve God, but him. "Wrath is cruel and anger is outrageous, but who is able to stand before envy?" (Prov. 27:4).

By introducing Adam to sin, through his lies, he succeeded in bringing man into bondage. The man and the woman were cast out of the Garden of Eden. "Therefore the Lord God sent him forth from the Garden of Eden, to till the ground from whence he was taken" (Gen. 3:23). However, God said to the serpent, "Because thou hast done this thou art cursed above all cattle, and above every beast of the field; upon thy belly shall thou go, and dust shall thou eat all the days of thy life: And I will put enmity between thee and the woman, and between thy seed and her seed; it shall bruise thy head, and thou shall bruise his heel" (Gen. 3:14-15). The stage was set for continuous war between God, the Serpent, the seed of Satan, and the seed of God. Who will rule and who will be worshipped?

The devil not only wanted worship from the angels and man, but he also wanted it from the only begotten Son of God: "And the devil, taking him [Jesus] into a high mountain, and showed unto him all the kingdoms of the world in a moment of time. And the devil said unto him, all this power will I give thee, and the glory of them: for that is delivered unto me: and to whomsoever I will I give it. [He offered it to Adam before and he took it.] If thou, therefore, will worship me, all shall be thine" (Lu.4:5-6).

He desires to be worshipped, and he hates man (a liar hates those that are afflicted by their lies Prov. 26:28), and for the exalted role that God gave to him. We know man is highly exalted in the sight of God because the Psalmist wrote, "What is man that thou art mindful of him; and the son of man that thou visited him? For thou hast made him a little lower than the angels, and hast crowned him with glory and honor. Thou madest him to have dominion over the works of thine hand: thou hast put all things under his feet." See also Gen 1:28.

Driven by envy and vain ambition, the devil wanted to be like the Almighty God. Isaiah prophesied of his vain desires saying, "For thou hast said in thine heart, I will ascend into heaven, I will exalt my throne above the stars of God: I will sit also upon the mount of the congregation, in the sides of the North: I will ascend above the heights of the clouds: I will be like the Most High" (Isa.14:13). Notice he wants to ascend into heaven, the place of God's eternal throne. He was in the Garden of Eden. He walked up and down upon the holy mountain amongst the stones of fire or the angels whose place is in heaven, but to sit on the throne in the heavenly Jerusalem; the kingdom of light and the power of holiness, is where Satan really wants to sit.

The Mother of Darkness

This is a section that I wrestled with for a long time. I had several revelations on this particular woman who was described to me as "evil." In my dreams I was either fighting against her, or being frustrated by her evil deeds. I wrote down the things I saw about her, but could not place her in any category. I saw her as the female head over the spirits of darkness. I saw her as a beautiful woman, or partly woman and partly animal. I saw her opposing the saints and waging war against them. I saw her as a human whose body was filled with nothing, but darkness. Then came the revelation that the woman is listed throughout the scriptures. I cannot tell whether her origin is part of the spirits of darkness that was left on earth, or whether her place is found in heaven. However, the Bible makes several references to a woman whom the apostle, John, saw with this name written on her forehead: "Mystery, Babylon The Great, The Mother of Harlots And Abominations Of The Earth." Rev.17:5. The word "mystery" is separated as if the woman herself is a mystery. However, she is the mother of the earth's abomination. Keep in mind that women are also represented as religious bodies. She also represents false religions, and is the source of religious power deeply rooted in darkness. She is also that seducing spirit that draws men away from right principals to spiritually fornicate with devils, and pervert their way.

Could this be the queen of heaven whom the children of Judah, and Israel, worshipped? When God was angry with them because of this sin, He said to Jeremiah, "The children gather wood, and the fathers kindle the fire, and the women knead their dough, to make cakes to the queen of heaven, and to pour out drink offerings unto other gods, that they may provoke me to anger." Jer. 7:18 what is obvious, is this deity, is not part of the Godhead in heaven.

However, the children of Israel felt that when they burned incense to her and made cakes for her, it went well with them. They burnt incense, poured out drink offerings and worshipped her and believed it was she who provided for them and protected them. God saw that as an abominable practice and an evil act which resulted in the desolation of the land, and the curse going forth, bringing death, destruction, and misery. (Jer.44:17-22). Can we conclude that this is the same woman, the queen of darkness who is described as the lady of the kingdoms? Who said, "I shall be a lady forever, . . . 'I shall not sit as a widow, neither shall I know the loss of children." Isa.47:5-8.

Some of her other qualities and ways are: she is given to pleasure and lives carelessly, She practices sorcery and enchantments, she also trust in her wickedness, and says, "None seeth me.' Isaiah, the prophet, wrote about her practices:" Stand now with thine enchantments, and with the multitude of thy sorceries, wherein thou hast labored from thy youth; . . . Thou art wearied in the multitude of thy counsels. Let now the astrologers, the star gazers, the monthly prognosticators stand up and save thee Isa. 47:810.

Upon closer examination we find some features about this woman, which mirror those of Satan. The prophet, Isaiah, wrote: "Thy wisdom and thy knowledge, it hath perverted thee; and thou hast said in thine heart, I am and none else besides me." Isa. 47:12-13. The king of Tyrus, was described in a similar way by the prophet Ezekiel. "Thine heart was lifted up because of thy beauty, thou has corrupted thy wisdom by reason of thy brightness." Eze. 28:17. The spirits of darkness that were placed in flesh were also male and female. At some point, Satan and this Woman began working together through the arm of flesh. They are both very wise and their spirits govern the darkness of the world. Satan controls the political governments, and she the religious. Her spiritual energy is in the earth, and she understands the movements of the constellations. She is served by those who practice witchcraft and every other abomination and filthiness. After God destroyed humans, except for Noah and his family, the spirit simply returned to the earth and inhabited other bodies. She, herself, no doubt can travel to and fro like Satan, between earth and heaven.

This is the same woman whom the prophet Zachariah wrote about whose resemblance was the same throughout the earth, "Wickedness." She was lifted up between the heaven and the earth, and was to be taken to the land of Shinar where the two women who flew her there was to set her down. Zech. 5:7-11. She must be sealed up for a season in her ephah, (a container the size of the person being place in it) "New Bible Dictionary Second Edition," J.D. Douglas et.all", until a permanent place is built for her. Satan must also be sealed up for a season. I saw these two as having a child together, Satan and this spirit that operates from darkness, will bring forth the son of perdition: "Even him, whose coming is after the working of Satan with all power and signs and lying wonders." 2 Thes. 2:9. This is the beast whom the dragon gives power, and who is carried by this woman whom John wrote about in the book of Revelations.

Darkness and Chaos Follows Satan's Legacy

Having opened the doors to the spirits of Death and Hell, Satan proceeded to deceive the whole world by introducing falsehood from the very beginning of time. The way to the knowledge of eternal life was hidden from man, and so the kingdoms of the world were built on falsehood crafted by Satan. "Shall the throne of iniquity have fellowship with thee, which frameth mischief by a law" (Psalms 94:20). The murderous spirit the world inherited is also from Satan. Our Lord and Savior, Jesus, described him as, "A murderer from the beginning, and abode not in the truth, [or the light] because there is no truth in him. When he speaketh a lie he speaketh of his own for he is a liar and the father of it" (John 8:44).

That murdering, lying spirit was first manifested through Cain who killed his brother Abel. Why did he kill him? Envy, pride, and greed are the spirit that operates in the children of disobedience who make up the kingdom of the world (Jude: 10-11). Satan had the power of death and kept Adam and his posterity in bondage through the fear of death (Heb2:15). Remember the wages of sin is death, and after Adam was cast out of the Garden, the way of the Tree of Life was kept from him. The devil and his host ruled with fear, lies, and oppression. All the thoughts and the imagination of man's heart was filled with wickedness after being introduced to sin, prompting God to destroy the world, saving only Noah who found grace in his eyes.

Hope

The battle lines have been drawn, and God has appointed a day when he will cast Satan down to earth by force. Ezekiel prophesied of that time saying, "I will cast thee as profane out of the mountain of God: and I will destroy thee, O covering Cherub, from the midst of the stones of fire. Thine heart was lifted up because of thy beauty, thou hast corrupted thy wisdom by reason of thy brightness: I will cast thee to the ground, I will lay thee before kings that they may behold thee" (Eze.28:17).

God will cast Satan down to earth as is stated in the book of Revelation: "And there was war in heaven: Michael and his angels fought against the dragon; and the dragon fought and his angels, and prevailed not; neither was their place found any more in heaven. And the great dragon was cast out, that old Serpent, called the Devil, and Satan, which deceived the whole world: he was cast out into the earth, and his angels were cast out with him." Rev. 12:7-8 He will permanently lose his place in heaven and finally exposed to the wrath of God through the body of Christ.

Now the time is yet to come when God's kingdom on earth will rule over all the kingdoms. Jesus came and took the keys of death away from the devil and has given us power over the powers of darkness. By his death and resurrection from the dead, he abolished death for those who believe in his name. We need no longer fear death, but avoid the sting of death which is sin. We were given power over all the power of the enemy by the grace of God through Jesus.

This book only reveals the spirits and how they operate so that the reader can make an informed choice in the direction in which they choose to go. In the books that follow, the identity of the nations and the people who will be possessed by these spiritual camps will be revealed. For now, I hope that I have made it clear that we wrestle not against flesh and blood, but against the spiritual forces that operate in high and low places. Man is not alone. He never was and never will be, but he must decide what camp or who he will serve. "See I have set before thee this day life and good, and death and evil" (Deut. 30:15).

Hell

Another group of angels and spirits are those who live under the earth. They are the evil angels and spirits who are in league with Satan, Death, and Hell. Hell is a place with life forms that are different from those on earth or heaven. From the book of Philippians, we learn, "That at the name of Jesus every knee shall bow, of things in heaven, and things in earth, and things under the earth" (Phil 2:10). So we know from that scripture that there are living creatures living there with the intelligence to bow before Jesus.

From the book of Revelation, we learn that there are also men there. "And no man in heaven, nor in earth, neither under the earth, was able to open the book, neither to look thereon" (Rev.5:3). Hell is the land of spirits and the throne of Death. Not all spirits of the dead go to hell. Some of the spirits of the dead live in hell. Others are under the throne of God waiting for the resurrection of the dead, and some are in the sea. "And the sea gave up the dead which was in it; and death and hell delivered up the dead which were in them" (Rev.20:13).

After Jesus died, the graves of the righteous were opened, and upon His resurrection, they came out of their graves and went in to the holy city. Those sprits who were once a captive of Death and Hell were free never to return to the land of darkness (Mark 27:52-53)

They, no doubt, are gone to be with the Lord and are living somewhere amongst the celestial bodies. These are probably the spirits of the good who had been made perfect and now reside in Zion. Then there are those dead who live in hell. They are conscious of their existence and are prisoners until the Day of Judgment. This we know from the prophet Ezekiel who wrote concerning Egypt and its multitude. "The strong among the mighty shall speak to him out of the midst of hell, with them that help him: they are gone down, they lie uncircumcised, slain by the sword" (Eze. 32:21). He also wrote; "For they are all delivered unto death, to the nether parts of the earth; in the midst of the children of men, with them that go down to the pit. Thus saith the Lord God; In the day when he went down to the grave I caused a mourning . . . I made the nations to shake at the sound of his fall, when I cast him down to hell with them that descended into the pit: and all the trees of Eden, the choice and the best of Lebanon, all that drink water shall be comforted in the nether parts of the earth. They also went down into hell with him" (Eze 31:14-17). The reader should note that the heathen are delivered to death, in a place called hell, which is also called the nether parts of the earth or the pit. (See also Eze 32:24-32).

The Location of Hell

Jesus called the land of the dead the heart of the earth, where he spent three days and three nights. "For as Jonah was three days and three nights in the whale's belly; so shall the Son of man be three days and three nights in the heart of the earth" (Matt. 12:40). There he ministered to the souls who were dead and kept as prisoners of Death and Hell. "For Christ also hath once suffered for sins, the just for the unjust, that he might bring us to God, being put to death in the flesh, but quickened by the Spirit. By which also he went and preached unto the spirits in prison" (1Pet.3:18-19).

Hell is located deep under the surface of the earth. This is also known as the pit where the uncircumcised and the wicked go. This is a land of darkness where the light is as darkness. This land described by Job as "the land of darkness and the shadow of death, a land of darkness, as darkness itself; and of the shadow of death, without any order, and where the light is or darkness" (Job 10:21-22). There is chaos, as Job said, and no order.

There are also torments and deprivation, for "the wicked shall be turned into hell, and all the nations that forget God. The torments of the wicked will be many in that land filled with wicked and evil creatures. Job said of the wicked, rich man: 'The rich man shall lie down, but he shall not be gathered; he openeth his eyes, and he is not. Terrors shall take hold on him as waters; a tempest stealeth him away in the night. The east wind carrieth him away, and he departeth; and as a storm hurleth him out of his place. For God shall cast upon him, and not spare" (Job 27:19-22).

Imagine for a moment you lying in the comfort of your fortress built by illegal or oppressive means. Then when you least expect it, you find yourself hurled down to a dark land. When you open your eyes, there is nothing but horrible sights before you, driving you from one terror to the other. The evil that you have done is constantly reminding you, for it is payback time. There is no escaping, and now you are like the troubled sea. "The wicked are like the troubled sea . . . there is no peace saith the Lord, unto the wicked" (Isaiah 48:22).

Jesus spoke this parable about this place called hell. In his parable, He compared hell to paradise where the righteous go after death. From hell, the wicked caught a glimpse of paradise. "And in hell he lift up his eyes being in torment and he cried and said Father Abraham have mercy on me and send Lazarus that he may dip the tip of his finger in water, and cool my tongue, for I am tormented in this flame" (Luke 16:25). So bitter was the experience for the man in hell that he wanted someone to warn his brothers to prevent them from going to such a dreadful and parched place.

Solomon said that at that point when those who had turned away from God reap their reward, they will cry out to God for help, but the answer is not very comforting.

"I also will laugh at your calamity; I will mock when your fear cometh; when your fear cometh as desolation and your destruction cometh as a whirlwind; when distress and anguish cometh upon you" (Prov.1:26-27). The flames of hell and its terrors are also mentioned by Job who describes what awaits the wicked when confronted with death. "He shall flee from the iron weapon, and the bow of steel shall strike him through. It is drawn, and cometh out of the body; yea, the glittering sword cometh out of his gall: terrors are upon him. All darkness shall hide in his secret places: a fire not blown shall consume him" (Job 20:25-26). Solomon and Job only speak of terror and anguish when writing about that dark and hot place.

Levels of Hell

Hell has different levels of torment. No doubt fear and anguish prevail there. The Psalmist praised God for delivering him from the lowest hell and warns those that seek to destroy him, that they "shall go into the lower parts of the earth" (Psalms 86:13, 63:9). That place where the spirits retain their consciousness as they descend downward. Ezekiel described an army descending into the pit as going to the low parts of the earth, to places desolate of old (Eze.26:20). For from hell, "the strong among the mighty shall speak to him out of the midst of hell" (Eze.32:21).

Jesus, in teaching about the seriousness of dying and going to this place, said to his disciples, "And if thy hand offends thee, cut it off: it is better for thee to enter into life maimed than having two hands to go into hell, into the fire that never shall be quenched. Where their worm dieth not and the fire is not quenched" (Mark 9:43-44). It is better to lose a part of your body than to lose your soul to hell's fire. Your worm or your spirit that never dies will be in torment in unquenchable fire. The soul retains a conscious knowledge of the life it lived.

Another example of the spirit retaining consciousness in hell is found in the book of Samuel. King Saul was desperate, and he needed to hear from God. God refused to talk to him, and so he went to a witch to raise the spirit of Samuel, the prophet, from the land of the dead. When Samuel was awakened, for he was asleep and ascended to the surface of the earth, he said to him: "'Why hast thou disquieted me, to bring me up?' And Saul answered, 'I am sore distressed; for the Philistines make war against me, and God is departed from me, and answered me no more, neither by prophets, nor by dreams: therefore I have called thee, that thou mayest make known to me what I shall do.' Then said Samuel, 'wherefore then dost thou ask of me, seeing the Lord is departed from thee, and is become thine enemy?' From the land of the dead Samuel proceeded to prophesy to Saul and reminded him why he was in that situation. Samuel was fully aware of his past actions and was able to predict his future. He prophesied that the next day Saul and his sons would join him in the land of the dead. 1Sam.28:8-19

That is a good example of how the spirits from the dead communicates with people in the land of the living. They are conscious and aware of their deeds in the past. I do not recommend that people should go to mediums and those who have familiar spirits because you leave yourself open to a host of devils. When you invite them as company to your home, do not be surprised if they don't want to leave, or if they bring along some of their buddies. Your iniquities will also go down to hell with you because they shall keep you a prisoner of death and hell. "And they shall not lie down with the mighty that are fallen or the uncircumcised, which are gone down to hell with their weapons of war: and they have laid their sword under their head, but their iniquities shall be upon their bones, though they were a terror in the land of the living" (Eze. 32:27). His own iniquities shall take hold of the wicked, and a man's unforgiving sins also keeps him locked up in hell. The sting of death is sin, and the strength of sin is God's law. It is better to have the victory over death and hell through Christ Jesus, than to go to the land of torments and terrors.

Finally, one day the keepers of hell will be loose on the earth to torment the wicked. John described these creatures as locust. He described them as horses prepared for battle with faces like those of men, women's hair, and lion's teeth. They also had wings. These creatures will be wearing iron breastplate, and their scorpion like tail will be used to sting people. Over them is a king, the angel of the bottomless pit, called, Abaddon (Rev.9:7-11). These will ascend from the pit in clouds of dust. As when a volcano erupts and spews out a cloud, so will their ascension to the earth's surface be. During the time of their plague on earth, man will seek death, but death will flee from them. If they will be so terrifying on earth, just think how terrible they are in their natural habitat.

My one vision of hell was that it was a land filled with darkness. I was going down through a crack in the earth. I was walking down on what looked like stairs that led me to a very dark land. It had a wall with a gate, and from a distance, I saw what looked like two people standing in front of the gate. The light behind the wall looked dark red, mixed with darkness. I did not want to get too close to the gate. The place had a sense of doom and gloom, and I did not want to be a prisoner nor a visitor. I figure that this land where death, creatures of darkness, evil, and wickedness resides must not be a very pleasant land, for, it is the home of evil, wicked, and unregenerate people. There they find neither rest nor peace. The population also consists of evil angels, devils, and creatures too numerous to mention. Death, rules over all that lives there, for that is his dominion. Death and Hell's interest on earth is for more souls. They are gathering souls into their kingdom. Are you one of them? You can decide today if hell is the place you want to be after you leave this earth. Jesus made a way for us to escape from death and hell by dying on the cross for our sins. Choose the better way.

CHAPTER SIX

First Seal

All prophetic dreams, visions, symbolic language, and that which the prophets and apostles foretold, must be in harmony. Each must be a witness to the other. This chapter attempts to open the readers' understanding of the seals mentioned throughout the Holy Bible, and especially those in the book of Revelation, as well as the prophecies that Daniel was told were sealed until the time of the end. How were they sealed? They were written in prophetic language filled with symbols. The only way for anyone to understand these prophetic symbols is through revelation from God. Isaiah wrote of a time of blindness that would come upon Israel. That time of blindness also represents the sealing of prophecy. "For the Lord hath poured out upon you the spirit of deep sleep, and hath closed your eyes: the prophets and your rulers, the seers hath he covered. And the vision of all is become unto you as the words of a book that is sealed, which men deliver to one that is learned, saying, Read this, I pray thee: and he saith, I cannot; for it is sealed: And the book is delivered to him that is not learned, saying, Read this, I pray thee: and he saith, I am not learned" (Isaiah 29:10-12, KJV). The Spirit of God will reveal the contents of His Word unto all mankind before fulfilling His word.

The book of Revelation is the most appropriate place to begin the prophetic journey. By listing the events in the sequence in which they were revealed to me; at the same time, showing the harmony of the revelations, with the other prophets, I hope to make prophecy easy to understand. The apostle John was taken to heaven and said, "And I saw in the right hand of him that sat on the throne a book written within and on the backside, sealed with seven seals" (Revelation 5:1, KJV). The prophet Daniel was told, "Go thy way, Daniel: for the words are closed up and sealed till the time of the end" (Daniel 12:9, KJV). The prophecies that seemed incomprehensible to Daniel were revealed to

John, the writer of the book of Revelation. They both saw far into the future, but only what was relevant to their generation could be fully understood by them. Prophecy that is sealed up is revealed to a prophet of the generation to which the message is relevant. This generation will hear and see the fulfillment of many prophecies that were sealed to be revealed to all nations at this time.

Daniel and John

Throughout the scriptures, we find that there is a harmony among the prophets. There are no contradictions, but rather a presentation of similar information in a different manner. Daniel and John had parallel experiences, and from both of them, the reader gets a clearer picture. Some of Daniel's visions gave some glimpses into the future. He foretold of the coming of Jesus, his death, triumph, and return to earth. Daniel saw him as the stone and the Messiah. From the time of Daniel's prophetic vision until the fulfillment thereof with the coming of Christ, no one saw clearly, but they waited patiently. When Christ came, he was not recognized by many who waited for him, yet the wise men saw his star, and it was revealed to the shepherds, Elizabeth, Zachariah, and those to whom the Lord revealed it. Daniel, also, saw the second coming of Christ, but again, he saw this without a clear understanding.

However, John, as is outlined in the book of Revelation, also saw the prophetic events that lead to Christ's second coming, his reign, and the end of this world.

Daniel and John had complimentary or supporting visions. All the prophets and apostles received the revelations of Daniel and John. As with Daniel, an angel of the Lord revealed the content of the prophetic visions to John. John was taken into heaven and had a heavenly guide walk him through the future while explaining to him the things he was seeing. One of the things he saw was a book that had seven seals. Upon seeing that no one on earth or in heaven or under the earth was worthy to open the book that was sealed, John began to weep. Then one of the elders said to him:

> Weep not: behold, the lion of the tribe of Judah, the Root of
> David, hath prevailed to open the book, and to loose the seals
> thereof. And I beheld, and, lo, in the midst of the throne and
> of the four beasts, and in the midst of the elders, stood a Lamb

as it had been slain, having seven horns and seven eyes, which
are the seven Spirits of God sent forth into all the earth. And
he came and took the book out of the right hand of him that
sat upon the throne. (Revelation 5:4-7, KJV)

When the Lion/Lamb opened the seals, John saw a sequence of
prophetic events that corresponded to Daniel's prophecies. It was
shown to John what would take place in the earth before the return of
the Lord. John's revelations start after Jesus' death, his burial, and his
resurrection. The prophecies from John did not go backward into time,
but showed the future. The identity of the nations discussed in John's
and Daniel's visions were kept hidden to be revealed in God's appointed
time because some of the nations did not exist at the time when they
received the visions, nor even today. They, as well as other prophets,
saw far into the future and wrote what they saw for us living today. The
information is to guide, instruct, and prepare this generation and the
subsequent generations for the things that are coming upon the earth.

Revelations from the Spirit of Truth

As I stated in an earlier chapter, the revelations of the contents of
the seals are revealed to this generation through the Holy Ghost moving
upon and through today's prophets whom God calls. No man can take
this honor upon himself. God has to call, and God has to reveal it. Jesus
told his disciples that he would send the Spirit of truth into the earth
that would guide us in all truth. Today we hear from this Spirit about the
things that are coming upon earth, as Jesus foretold. "Howbeit when he,
the Spirit of truth, is come, he will guide you into all truth: for he shall
not speak of himself; but whatsoever he shall hear, that shall he speak:
and he will show you things to come. He shall glorify me: for he shall
receive of mine, and shall show it unto you. All things that the Father
hath are mine: therefore said I that he shall take of mine, and shall show
it unto you." (John 16:13-16, KJV)

Daniel and Jeremiah

Daniel's visions, which are closely linked to John's visions, give us a
detailed glimpse into the future. Daniel's prophecies differ from John's
in that they included the coming of the Messiah, and his prophesies help
the reader to establish a time line. Daniel, also, saw the second coming

of Christ, but again, he saw this without understanding. As Daniel was praying and seeking an understanding of Jeremiah's seventy-year period of captivity, the angel of the Lord came to him and said, "Seventy weeks are determined upon thy people and upon thy holy city, to finish the transgression and to make reconciliation for iniquity, and to bring everlasting righteousness, and to seal up the vision and prophesy and to anoint the Most Holy" (Dan.9:24).

After the Babylonian captivity, those prophecies were not all fulfilled. The angel also spoke of a time after the seventy-year Babylonian captivity period, a time when everlasting righteousness will be established on the earth. Daniel's seventy-week period that relates to the time of the end was to me a mystery and very confusing. At first, I tried to relate it to Jeremiah's prophecy about the seventy years of Babylonian captivity and sought for some type of similitude. There are some similarities, but they are not the same prophesies. The prophet Daniel was also praying and studying the scriptures with the hope of understanding Jeremiah's seventy-year prophecies of the captivity of his people. However, he found out through the angel that Jeremiah's seventy years was more than just a period of captivity intended only for the Jews, but also a blueprint of the time marking the end. Without divine guidance, the mysteries of the scriptures are hidden in a language that only God can reveal. This is what was revealed to me concerning the seventy weeks. Daniel's seventy weeks dealt with a twofold prophecy, the state of Israel, represented as the Jews at Sinai, and the church, the spiritual people who were redeemed by the blood of Jesus, and born of the Spirit, through faith in Jesus Christ.

God's Divine Plan

After Jesus came and walked the earth, Jerusalem at Sinai did not see the fulfillment of all of Daniel's prophecies especially not as it relates to the church. A new nation and people, or a seed, was planted in the earth that we call the Lamb's Bride. However, that body composed of all nations, Jews, and Gentiles, needed to grow and develop into a perfect man in the earth (Eph.2). The apostle Paul referred to this body as the Israel of God, and the members as the true Jew whose circumcision is in the heart, who serve God in spirit and in truth (Rom. 2:28). This nation of people were scattered throughout the earth in order for God to form it from people of every race, nationality, and religion. As seed that is sown grows in different locations of a field under different circumstances, so the body of believers belonging to this new nation has grown on the earth. That was just one phase of God's divine plan.

The church must go through a prophetic seventy-year period where the members will come together and the kingdom of God, represented as the New Man, will be fully formed in the earth. That period will include the rise and fall of nations embracing the Christian faith, as well as the nations of the world that will come against them, as God call all nations to the obedience of the faith. Nations will struggle against this kingdom that will rule over all kingdoms and nations. The people from this kingdom look to heavenly Jerusalem who is the mother of us all and not to Jerusalem at Sinai (Gal.4:22-26). Daniel Seventy weeks relates to the rise of this kingdom and the sequence of events that will take place during that specific period.

The State of the Church

Today there are no apparent walls to stem the flow of all the varying, and damaging doctrines, coming into the church, or going out of the church. The walls must be built, and the spiritual house restored. The foundation that Jesus laid cannot be laid again, but many has taken it upon themselves to promote perverse doctrines in the name of the church. The building or the body in which the Holy Spirit desires to reside, must be built into a spiritual house, worthy to offer up praises to God. Jesus said, "If I be lifted up from the earth, I will draw all men unto me". Jesus must first be formed in the earth and then lifted up from the earth. The laws of God must be looked upon as: good, and just, and righteous, filled with justice and truth.

The house will be completed after the fulfillment of Ezekiel's vision of the dry bones coming together to form a holy army in the earth. There must also be a great outpouring of the Holy Ghost after a period of mass conversion. There must also follow a persecution and the great falling away. Daniel's seventy years covers those events that must take place with the church. The broken walls of the church are manifested by the current state of the church. There are many contrary and contradicting voices today claiming to represent Christ. God's moral and righteous laws are being forced out of the church, and His grace is used as an occasion for sin. Yet God stated that his laws will be established for ever in heaven and earth. God's divine plan and purpose as interpreted by various denominations clearly suggest that among the faithful, there are conflicting and opposing views that foster the divisions amongst the believers. There are also those who are of the church that Satan set up to distract the unsuspecting and lead them away. The wheat and the tare's parable is a good example of that. (Math. 13: 24-30)

Greed is rampant by rulers of corrupt minds whose intentions are devilish, and they themselves are instruments of Satan. The standards have fallen to unacceptable lows, and the *house of God is become a den of thieves*. Some things that God clearly called unacceptable and abominable in His church that he purchased with His own blood, is now embraced and preached as acceptable and practiced by some religious leaders professing to be Christians. These are found in various denominations. No need to marvel. Satan does disguise himself as an angel of light and so also does his disciples. The enemy hath planted some of those churches amongst the true church of God. It is true that the wheat and the tare must grow together, and by their fruits we shall know them. However, the silence concerning the abominable practices, in the current state of the church, from the rest of the sanctified ones who know the truth, is sometimes deafening, but the divine plan is unfolding as God said it would.

God's plan is to complete the body of Christ in the earth. This body will be presented to Christ as the bride of the Lamb wearing garments without spots and wrinkles. This body, along with sanctified Jews, will God unite in the earth into one body, and give them one shepherd. However, the cleansing and preparation comes with much trials and tribulations. That period of building the wall in troublous times will be very challenging for those who will take the lead to build the walls. The prophecy about Jerusalem at Sinai directly ties into the prophecies about the church. Jesus is the only way to the Father and through His cross we are all Christians, or spiritual Jews.

CHAPTER SEVEN

The Time of the End

From the book of Daniel, we get a prophetic time line that lists certain events and the amount of time it will take for those events to be fulfilled. Those events put us within range of the year when Jesus' return to earth will take place. The book of Zechariah talks of the season of the year when His return will happen. In the book of Acts, we read that all things concerning Jesus must be fulfilled. Jesus speaking to his disciples spoke of things being fulfilled within the lifetime of a generation. Then speaking in a timeless manner, Jesus warns, "Do not be as the hypocrites who can discern the face of the sky, but cannot discern the signs of the times" (Matthew 16:3, KJV).

With all the information provided by the prophets and holy apostles, including our Lord Jesus and the Spirit of truth guiding us in all truth, the faithful has a prophetic view into the future, with clear signs to follow that leads to the very season of the return of the Lord. The day and the hour we do not know, but we were given the times and the season. This time line and the events associated with them will be explained in detail as the Lord has revealed them to me as we go through this work. It was revealed to me that seventy years is the amount of time that it will take to fulfill the prophecies written in the Seven Seals. Those scriptures listed above are showing what will take place toward the end, but the end has a dramatic beginning, a dark and dreary middle, and a bloody and grand finale.

The last seven years are the ones most widely discussed amongst the religious and the scholars. There is often heated discussions as to which will come first—the rapture or the tribulation, neither of which most people alive today will live to see. The debates continue with some claiming that the Lord will return any minute or any day. Hopefully, as the Spirit guides us through the scriptures, we all will get a better understanding of what the Lord's intentions are and His divine plan for His people.

As stated before, the prophecies revealed throughout the Bible are in harmony and consistent with one another, including those that Jesus shared with His disciples. Jesus gave us certain clear signs to follow, that are in line with Daniel's prophesies as well as in line with the content of the Seven Seals identified by John in the book of Revelation, and throughout the Bible.

Jesus Warns His Disciples

The disciples curiously asked of Jesus when the end should come. "Tell us, when shall be the sign of thy coming, and of the end of the world?" (Matthew 24:3, KJV) Jesus proceeded to tell them all the things that were to happen without giving details, but giving the sequential order of these events. After listing the sequence of events, He made it clear to them that this was the way in which the events would unfold.

Jesus lists a sequence of events must be accomplished before the great day of His return in the sky to gather the remnant unto Him. His disciples ask two questions, when and what? Jesus answered and said unto them, "Take heed that no man deceives you. For many shall come in my name, saying, I am Christ; and shall deceive many. And ye shall hear of wars and rumors of wars: see that ye be not troubled: for all these things must come to pass; but the end is not yet. All these are the beginning of sorrows" (Matthew 23:3-8). The things we read, see, and hear are only events that are shaping the future to bring us to that time.

Some other things that must happen and that we often see are that nations will rise up against nations, kingdom against kingdom, earthquakes and other natural disasters in different places, famines, and social and political unrest and troubles. Before Christ returns there will be persecutions, unjust trials, and beatings. The gospel also must be preached amongst all nations. Some of those who accept Jesus as Lord will be betrayed by their family members who will have some of them put to death. There will be upheavals in the home and in the communities. Religious and racial cleansing will take place on a scale never before seen. The sun will be darkened, and the moon will not shine figuratively, referring to the times when preaching will neither be permitted nor possible. It will also take place literally. There will be great signs from heaven, and men's hearts will fail when they see the evil that is coming upon the earth. The powers of heaven shall also be shaken. There will be wars on earth, in heaven, and under the earth as this period comes to a close. All those things will take place in that order during the seventy years of the end.

The Last Seven

The first three and a half years of the last seven years of the seventy-year period will be brutal for Christians. The world reel from the violence and debauchery that will stain it with blood. Jesus told his disciples to read Daniel's prophecy about the seventy weeks for a sign. He said to his disciples, "And ye shall be hated of all men for my name's sake: but he that shall endure unto the end, the same shall be saved. But when ye shall see the abomination of desolation, spoken of by Daniel the prophet, standing where it ought not, [let him that readeth understand] then let them that be in Judea flee to the mountains. For in those days shall be affliction, such as was not from the beginning of the creation which God created unto this time, neither shall be. But in those days, after that tribulation, the sun shall be darkened, and the moon shall not give her light" (Mark 13:14-20). Luke adds, "And when ye shall see Jerusalem compassed with armies then know that the desolation thereof is nigh . . . For these be the days of vengeance that all things which were written may be fulfilled . . . And they (Jews), shall fall by the edge of the sword, and shall be led away captive into all nations; and Jerusalem shall be trodden down by the Gentiles, until the times of the Gentiles be fulfilled . . . So likewise ye, when ye see these things come to pass, know ye that the kingdom of God is nigh at hand" (Lu 23:8-31). Jerusalem will be surrounded with armies after the abomination of desolation spoken of by Daniel, will stand in the holy place, but Christians will see that take place before they are redeemed.

When that happens, Jesus said, "Look up because your redemption is near." That verse relates to the last three and a half years of the seventy years, and will conclude the end of the Gentile age. This we know from John, who wrote, "But the court which is without the temple leave out, and measure it not; for it is given unto the Gentiles: and the holy city shall they thread under foot forty and two months" (Rev 11:2).

We also read about the two witnesses, who shall prophesy a thousand two hundred and threescore days during the last these last years. They are a sign for the Jews, to measure the time of the end. At the end of their prophecy, they are called up to heaven, but only after the seventh angel blow the last trumpet. (Rev. 11: 2, 11). There are other sign we will follow as we go through the prophecies relating to the end of this age. However, the last years are clearly described with length of time associated with the prophecy. Daniel was told by the angel, "And from the time that the daily sacrifice is taken away, and the abomination that maketh desolate set up, there shall be a thousand three hundred and ninety days. Blessed is he that waiteth,

and cometh to the thousand three hundred and five and thirty days."
Dan. 12:11-12. The time is never exact, but the seasons are sure. The
Lord could delay his coming, or come in an hour when we are not
expecting, but the seasons must be fulfilled. However, we calculate the
last three and a half to four years base on the sequential events and
the duration of time given to them.

In the book of Revelation we read about a beast that was given power
to make war with the saints and to overcome them. "And there was given
unto him a mouth speaking great things and blasphemies; and power
was given unto him to continue forty and two months" (Rev. 13:5).
Daniel was also told, "And he shall confirm the covenant with many for
one week: and in the midst of the week he shall cause the sacrifice and
oblation to cease, and for the overspreading of abominations he shall
make it desolate, even until the consummation, and that determined
shall be poured upon the desolate" (Dan.9:27). Those two events, which
are the same, help us to understand Daniel's seventy weeks. We can
conclude that a prophetic week equals seven years as it relates to the
end. Daniel was seeking the lord concerning the seventy-year prophecy
of Jeremiah when he received that revelation. (Dan.9:2).

Jeremiah's Vision

The prophet Jeremiah foresaw some of what would take place
during the end of the age and wrote about the last seventy years. He
first establishes that what is coming is the Lord's doing. "Behold the
whirlwind of the Lord goeth forth with fury, a continuing whirlwind:
it shall fall with pain upon the head of the wicked. The fierce anger
of the Lord shall not return, until he hath done it, and until he has
performed the intents of his heart: in the latter days ye shall consider it"
(Jer 23:19,20).

Jeremiah foresaw the destruction that was coming upon the whole
world when the Lord begins to pour out his fury

Jeremiah was also told to prophesy, saying, "The Lord shall roar from
on high, and utter his voice from his holy habitation; he shall give a
shout, as they that tread the grapes, against all the inhabitants of the
earth. A noise shall come even to the ends of he earth; for the Lord hath
a controversy with the nations, he will plead with all flesh; he will give
them that are wicked to the sword, saith the Lord. Thus saith the Lord
of host, Behold evil shall go forth from nation to nation and a great
whirlwind shall be raised up from the coast of the earth and the slain of
the Lord shall be at that day from one end of the earth even unto the

other end of the earth: they shall not be lamented, neither gathered, nor buried, they shall be dung upon the ground (Jer. 25:32-33).

Jeremiah saw what the lord will do to the nations and the extent of His judgment upon some specific nations. The anger of the Lord will affect all nations as He pours out His fury upon the head of the wicked. Those times will affect both the just and the unjust, and nowhere on earth will be a place to escape. Some will have it harder than others, but the world must prepare to meet its maker. The whole world will be affected by war, occupation of countries by foreign governments, terrorism, sedition, and upheavals. Famines and natural disasters, plagues, and diseases never before seen will come upon the earth. Science will seek to answer with so-called breakthroughs, but like when Moses confronted Egypt, the magicians came to one conclusion, so also will the scientist eventually conclude that this is the hand of God.

Personal Revelations

Thus far we have mainly covered the events that will take place during the last three and a half to seven years. Before going further into the various signs to look for about what the prophets wrote concerning the end, there are certain events that I must share with the readers. These events will directly affect the church, and whatever effects the church to a large extends will affect the world. We are the light of the world. The city that is set upon a hill when well lit cannot be hidden. We are also referred to as the salt of the earth, which keeps the world salted. When we lose our saltiness, we become good for nothing, but to be cast out. The church of God will go through a seventy-year period that will establish it as the well-lit city on the hill, as was shown to me.

In a dream, the Lord showed me that the seventy-year period will be broken down into ten seven-year periods. The United States as it was shown to me, is very interrelated in prophecies concerning the church. The reader will find that this country is used as a time marker for the church. I suppose that is because of the strength of the body of believers in this country and the special anointing and calling that is prepared for this nation.

At the beginning of the seventy-year period, I saw the United States as a nation sliding downward morally and economically into darkness. As it slid, I saw it miraculously turned around, and a period of great light followed. During that period of light, truth will abound and mysteries will unfold concerning prophecy, and the knowledge of God will increase. That period is when a messenger of truth will come forth filled with the power of the Holy Ghost. During that time, the church will grow exponentially, which will also be a period of spiritual and material growth and prosperity. The church growth will directly impact, and permanently change this nation.

After, the period of great prosperity, and evangelism, there will follow a time of cross darkness. This will be a very drought-stricken and war-torn period. This period leads into the spilling of much blood and global carnage. That period was followed by another period where light of the Holy Ghost shone dimly through the darkness. This period extended into several years where major prophecies will be fulfilled. Towards the end of that dark period I saw another period involving a great outpouring of the Holy Ghost. The whole world was filled with the Spirit of God. Then after that period, darkness gradually began to descend from the north and spread across the world to overtake the light. The darkness sought to cover the light, which endured throughout the rest of the time, even after I saw the church taken away, and the remnant remained in the light of the Holy Ghost on earth. Those periods of will lead us to the fulfillment of the seventy years.

During one of those seven years, I saw in the visions and dreams blood dripping upon the earth. What began in one corner quickly spread throughout the rest of the world, until the whole world was covered in blood. Toward the end of the Gentile age, I saw the seas become progressively more boisterous, and the waves beat with greater intensity against the rocks and at times flooded the lands surrounded by them. That will be a time of gross darkness, when millions of lives will be lost.

Every nation on the earth will be affected, and I saw that the sea spawned four cyclones. What was revealed to me is that four kingdoms will come forth with destructive fury, during the seventy-year time line. The world will go through major political and military shifts because of the four kingdoms that will come out of the sea. During the last years, I saw the waters beat furiously against the shores, and the rocks, representing the intensity of trouble. The waves were huge, and it was a frightful site to look at. The waters, the waves, nor the cyclones were able to completely cover the rocks that were in the water and on the shores, but they beat against it with great intensity. The light of God will never be completely taken out of the earth, for there will always be a group of people who will do righteously until all things are fulfilled and Christ returns triumphantly to the earth. I also saw great signs in the sky as I found shelter under a big tree. Standing for truth and calling on Jesus' name as we near the end, will not be without a fight as we face some dark and frightening days. Now let us follow the scriptures to go to the beginning of the seventy years and work our way back to the last three and a half years.

Nebuchadnezzar Dreams of the End-Time Prophecies

To understand the Seven Seals written in the book of Revelations, it is necessary to begin with Nebuchadnezzar's dream. The following is a chronological history of Nebuchadnezzar's dreams and the interpretation by Daniel. This is significant to note because from those prophesies, we can go directly into what this book is about, end-time prophecies. The history that led up to the Babylonian captivity is good to follow because God spoke through the prophets using similitude's to describe what would come to pass in the future. We read of the Prophet Jeremiah's seventy-year captivity, beginning with the reign of Nebuchadnezzar, the king of Babylon.

One night, the king of Babylon was pondering the future and questioning what the end should be. The Lord spoke to him in a dream in answer to his questions. However, he could not remember his dream, so he sent for the wise men of the kingdom, but they were not able to tell him his dream. Then Daniel came before the king and told him what he dreamed and gave him the interpretation.

Daniel proceeded to tell the dream and to interpret it. In his dream, the king saw a great image whose head was made of fine gold. The breast and the arms were of silver, the belly and thigh were brass, the legs of iron, and the feet part were made of iron and part clay. Beginning with the head of gold, Daniel began the interpretation by saying, "You, O king are a king of kings. For the God of heaven has given you a kingdom, power, strength, and glory; and wherever the children of men dwell, or the beasts of the field and the birds of the heaven, he has given them into your hand, and has made you ruler over them all. You are this head of gold. But after you shall arise another kingdom inferior to yours; then another, a third kingdom of bronze, which shall rule over the earth. And the fourth shall be strong as iron, inasmuch as iron breaks in pieces and shatters everything; and crush all the others. Whereas you saw the feet and toes, partly of potter's clay and partly of iron, the kingdom shall be divided; yet the strength of iron shall be in it, just as you saw the iron mixed with ceramic clay. And as the toes of the feet were partly of iron and partly of clay, so the kingdom shall be partly strong and partly fragile." Dan.2:29-42

The dream has two parts. That part of the dream and the interpretation only concerned the nations of the world and the kingdoms of man. However, the next part of the dream was about another kingdom made without hands, which was not left to man. Daniel continued, "As you saw iron mixed with ceramic clay, they will mingle with the seed of men; but they will not adhere to one another, just as iron does not, when mixed with clay. And in the days of these kings, the God of heaven will set up a kingdom which shall never be destroyed; and the kingdom shall not be left to other people; it shall break in pieces and consume all these kingdoms, and it shall stand forever. Inasmuch as you saw that the stone was cut out of the mountain without hands, and that it broke in pieces the iron, the bronze, the clay, the silver, and the gold, the great God has made known to the king what will come to pass after this. The dream is certain, and its interpretation is sure" (Dan.2:27, 31-45).

What Was Fulfilled?

History supports the scriptures by leaving evidence of prophecy fulfilled. We know the image began with Nebuchadnezzar; he was the head of gold (Dan. 2:38). King Nebuchadnezzar's Babylon was followed by Darius of Media Persia. The Medes and the Persians were the arm and breast of silver (Dan.5:27-31). The Medes and the Persians were followed by the Grecian Empire, which was the belly and thighs of brass. How do we now this? Daniel wrote that in the third year of Cyrus, king of Persia, a thing was revealed unto him. Then an angel came and spoke to him and said to him, "And now will I return to fight with the prince of Persia: and when I am gone forth, lo, the prince of Grecia shall come" (Dan.10:1, 20). That is also supported by historical documents that Alexander the Great did conquer that region and did set up the Grecian Empire.

The Roman Empire followed Greece as the divided kingdom whose feet and toes were part of potter's clay and part of iron. It was during the time of this empire that the prophecy says that God would set up his everlasting kingdom, which was cut out of the mountains without hands, and the stone would break in pieces the image that Nebuchadnezzar saw. The stone that Nebuchadnezzar saw struck the image on its feet, which was of iron and clay, and became a great kingdom, which would never be destroyed.

A reasonable question would be, who or what is the stone, and where is the mountain today? From the scriptures, we learned that Jesus is the stone whose kingdom was set up during the time of Roman rule. The light of Israel, the Son of God, was manifest in the earth and told Peter, one of his disciples, "Upon this Rock I build my church and the gates of hell shall not prevail against it." Jesus also spoke of the mustard seed, not just as the indication of the amount of faith one should have, but to illustrate how the kingdom of God was planted in the earth. "The kingdom of heaven is likenend to a grain of mustard seed, which a man took and sowed in his field: which indeed is the least of all seeds: but when it is grown, it is the greatest amongst the herbs, and becometh a tree, so that the birds of the air come and lodge in the branches thereof" (Mat. 13:31-32). The mountain or the seed, which will grow into a kingdom on earth is the stone that will become a great mountain.

The kingdom of God is continuing to grow in numbers and in stature. One day, it will rule over all the kingdoms of the world. Let us examine the stone a bit more. Jesus is the living stone, "disallowed indeed of men, but chosen of God and precious." (1 Pet.2:4). Paul also called him the Spiritual Rock from which the children drank in the wilderness. "And that Rock was Christ" (1Cor. 10:4). He is the shepherd and stone of Israel (Gen. 49:24). Finally, Zechariah wrote of him as the stone before Joshua that had seven eyes (Zech. 3:9).

Jesus the Stone

Let us examine the stone a bit more. Jesus is the living stone, "disallowed indeed of men, but chosen of God and precious" (1 Pet.2:4). Paul also called him the Spiritual Rock from which the children drank in the wilderness; "and that Rock was Christ" (1Cor. 10:4). He is the shepherd and stone of Israel (Gen. 49:24). Finally, Zachariah wrote of him as the headstone which cried, "Grace, grace, grace."

Before Jesus began his ministry, John the Baptist came preaching, "Repent ye: for the kingdom of heaven is at hand." John came preaching repentance and said to the people who followed him, "I indeed baptize you with water unto repentance: but he that cometh after me is mightier than I, whose shoes I am not worthy to bear: he shall baptize you with the Holy Ghost and with fire: whose fan is in his hand, and he will thoroughly purge his floor, and gather his wheat into the garner; but he will burn up the chaff with unquenchable fire" (Math. 3:2, 11-12).

John foresaw the kingdom of God and its coming with power. However, this was a spiritual kingdom that came not with observation. It was not what the people living in Palestine expected. Of this kingdom, Paul wrote, "The kingdom of God is not in word, but in power" (1 Cor.4:20). He also said that his preaching was not with eloquent speech, but with the demonstration of power by the Holy Ghost. Since the day of Pentecost that started with about one hundred and twenty disciples in the upper room, the church has grown into a multitude without number, a multitude from every nation.

Jesus made a clear differentiation between God's kingdom and those of the world when he told the Pharisees, "But if I cast out devils by the Spirit of God, then the kingdom of God is come unto you" (Math. 12:28). The Spirit of God, within us is what enables us to demonstrate the power of God, over all the power of Satan's kingdom. This is the kingdom Jesus established amongst the nations, a body of spiritual people united through water and Spirit baptism, and having a common faith and Lord (John 3:3-5). The Psalmist declares their glory saying, "Let the high praises of God be in their mouth and a two-edged sword in their hand to execute vengeance upon the heathen, and punishments upon the people; to bind their kings with chains, and their nobles with fetters of iron; to execute upon them the judgment written: this honor have all his saints. Praise ye the Lord" (Psalms 149:5-9). We praise God for the honor of calling us out of darkness, and making us a part of the kingdom of light to rule over the heathen and to establish truth and righteousness in the earth. The people of the kingdom are spiritual people who manifest through their flesh the glory and power of God. However, the fullness of the kingdom and the time when it will fully reign over the earth for a thousand years will be after the end of the seventy-year period. However, there will be a time before the return of the Lord, when the people of God will rule over the earth. This brief period, is a foretaste of what is to come.

Peter wrote that the kingdom God will establish is "a holy nation, a royal priesthood, a chosen generation, to show forth the praises of him who had called us out of darkness into the marvelous light" (1 Pet. 2:9). The members are princes and princesses, priests and prophets. This is the inheritance of the saints. This kingdom as was prophesied by Daniel will remain forever, eternal. Jesus also told Peter, "Upon this rock I build my Church and the gates of hell shall not prevail against it" Math 16:18. The process began with the stone striking the image. It will end when it fills the earth.

Did the Stone Already Strike the Image?

The question should be asked, did the stone strike the image and fill the earth? Or are we still like the grain of the mustard seed sowed into the earth, growing into a tree, and is still growing, filling the earth with a people to whom Paul wrote, "The God of peace shall bruise Satan under your feet shortly" (Rom.16:20). This is a mystery, which from the beginning of the world, had been hid in God, who created all things by Jesus Christ (Eph. 3:9). Jesus, for all who would believe on him, conquered death and "spoiled principalities and powers, and made a show of them openly, triumphing over them" (Col. 2:15).

After resurrecting from the dead, he gave the church power over all the power of the enemy as is written, "Behold I give unto you power to tread on serpents and scorpions, and over all the power of the enemy; and nothing shall by any means hurt you" (Lu. 10:19). Peter was also told, "Whatsoever you bind on earth shall be bound in heaven, and whatsoever you loosed on earth shall be loosed in heaven" (Math 16:16). This authority and power comes with the baptism of the Holy Ghost and is granted to the saints. Before they received the power to preach the gospel of the resurrection, Jesus commanded his disciples to go wait in Jerusalem until they receive the baptism of the Holy Ghost. Then they were to go into the entire world and preach the gospel to every creature, calling them to the obedience of the faith. So the kingdom came with Jesus, but was transferred to the apostles when the Spirit of truth filled each believer with power to live righteous and holy. That is why it is written, "For the kingdom of God is not meat and drink; but righteousness, and peace, and joy in the Holy Ghost" (Rom.14:17).

Now God had appointed a day in which he would judge the world in righteousness by the man Jesus and those joined to him, who are being gathered into one body in the earth. They are gathered by the Spirit of God and through the preaching and teachings of His word. Satan, in killing the Lord Jesus, fulfills the parable of the corn of wheat, for from the death of one, it grew into many. Through the death of Jesus, God multiplied the people who will rule over the earth. Everything that Nebuchadnezzar saw was fulfilled, except this part: "But it shall break in pieces and consume all these kingdoms, and it shall stand forever" (Dan. 2:44). The stone, which was set up during the days of those kingdoms, will soon break in pieces the kingdoms of the world by the people who are gathered in Christ. Jesus came into the world not only to save man from sin and give us the hope of eternal life; he also came to save us from the wrath to come.

CHAPTER EIGHT

Personal Revelation of the First Seal

The opening of the first seal will signal one of the greatest spiritual revolutionary events that this current generation will experience. There will be a period of great prosperity and blessings for the church at large, and many will turn to and convert to religion seeking answers and direction. This will be particularly true for Christianity. With the opening of the first seal a cry will go out calling for holiness and truth in Christian churches, and justice and righteousness throughout the world. Christian churches will go through a phenomenal period of growth, reorganization, and change. The whole world will be impacted by what will take place in the Kingdom of God. The following dreams and visions are some of the things I saw as they relate to the church with the opening of the first seal. In some of my dreams and visions from the Lord, I saw multitudes of people drawn by the Spirit of God and by the power of God into one body. The Spirit of God was unifying the church. That was followed by an outpouring of the Spirit of God upon the body. I saw how the young people were drawn to Christ in great numbers. I saw them as schools of fish moving in the direction in which the spirit was leading them. The unity among the believers came because it was the Spirit of God who was bringing this great number of people together.

The world will acknowledge the power of the Lord because there will be mighty signs, wonders, and unexplainable miracles to convince them all, that it is the power of God at work. The gathering of the people was throughout the western world, but the United States of America and Africa, including the land of Palestine, is where I saw the greatest manifestation of power. The United States is where the global revival will begin. That was followed by Africa and then some parts of eastern and western Europe.

The Executer of Justice

The opening of the first seal also signifies a period of conquest in the natural world. God is going to possess the earth, and the Spirit of God, through his servants, will call all nations to the obedience of the faith. For David prophesied, saying; "The Lord is known, by the judgment which he executed: the wicked is snared in the work of his own hands. The wicked shall be turned into hell and all nations that forget God. For the needy shall not always be forgotten: the expectation of the poor shall not perish forever. Arise o Lord; let not man prevail: let the heathen be judged in thy sight. Put them in fear O lord that the nations may know themselves to be but men" (Psalms 9:16-20). Throughout the world, the call to righteousness will go forth. The poor and needy people will see the light of hope and the answer to many tears and prayers on the horizon. The spirit of the rider who is released with the opening of the first seal will inhabit a body of believers who will go forth in righteousness to wage war. The elders written of in the book of Revelation who sat before God's throne in heaven, described the rider and the body that follows him, as they bowed to worship and sang this song to Jesus:

"Thou art worthy to take the book, and to open the seals thereof. For thou wast slain, and hast redeemed us to God by thy blood out of every kindred, and tongue, and people, and nation; and hast made us unto our God kings, and priest, and we shall reign on the earth" (Revelation 5:9-10, KJV). All nations, tongues, and cultures shall be brought into subjection by him and the body he is forming in the earth. He is the only one who can unlock the prophetic time clock. Once it begins, it cannot stop until all things are fulfilled.

"And I saw when the Lamb opened one of the seals, and I heard, as it were the noise of thunder, one of the four beasts saying, 'Come and see.' And I saw, and behold a white horse: and he that sat on him had a bow: and a crown was given unto him: and he went forth conquering and to conquer" (Revelation 6:1-2, KJV).

The mission of the first rider is to wage war and to conquer. The wars are both spiritual and carnal. The armies are God's children who will stand for truth and justice throughout the world. These do not possess a hidden agenda, but are God's instruments of righteousness who are led by the Spirit of God going forth conquering and to conquer. The Lord Jesus, speaking of the Spirit that was to come into the world after his resurrection, told his disciples, "And when he is come, he will reprove the world of sin, and of righteousness, and of judgment" (John 16:8).

It is the Spirit of truth expressed duty, not only to guide us in all truth, but also to judge the prince of this world. God will rise up his people as a mighty army and use them to judge the heathen. Jesus Christ our Lord and Savior, is the head of that body, which God had chosen to rule the earth with Him in Glory.

The elders, angels, and all that were in heaven glorified Jesus because of His obedience to the death of the cross, and to him is given glory, power, and dominion. Every creature in heaven, earth, even under the earth, and those that are in the sea will bow to him because this was God's promise to him.

"Wherefore God also hath highly exalted him, and given him a name which is above every name. That at the name of Jesus every knee should bow, of things in heaven, and things in earth, and things under the earth; and every tongue should confess that Jesus Christ is Lord, to the glory of God the Father" (Philippians 2:8-11, KJV).

This promise is also given to us, those of us who make up His body. He is the living Word that became flesh. He personified the Word and power of God to all men. So are we called to personify the Word and power of God to all men. So then, if we are one with Him in Spirit and Body, we are also one with Him as He goes forth "conquering and to conquer."

Being guided by the Spirit of God, the church will go forth with the Word of God preaching the gospel of salvation. God will confirm His Word with miracles, healings and deliverances, mighty signs, and wonders in all parts of the world. As the gospel of salvation is preached, people will be warned to flee from the terrible judgments that are coming to the wicked. The house of God will be a place of refuge, a shelter in those times of trouble and anguish. As a lighthouse in the world of darkness, the Christian light will shine to give hope and direction. As Christ is lifted up, many will come to the Lord, be converted, and be healed.

Symbols of the First Seal Identified and Explained

Visions will help us get an understanding of the Holy Scriptures. These are like prophetic keys to the Bible that unlock the hidden mysteries shown to the prophets. Through the writing of the prophets, we find a symbolic language. Every symbol represents people, places, and powers whose identities were sealed from the writing prophet but appointed for revelation in these last times. The power and awesomeness of God will be made manifest as he brings to pass things written thousands of years ago. The symbols must not be looked upon as static but as unfolding mysteries.

The language is common among all the prophets so that every word of God becomes important. Every piece of prophecy fits into the puzzle to clarify the will and purpose of God. For example, the prophet Zechariah had a vision, similar to that of John the Revelator. The symbols were different, yet his vision helps to explain the symbols of the book of Revelation. The angel that was speaking to Zechariah asked him, "'what seest thou?' He answered, 'And I said, I have looked, and behold a candlestick all of gold, with a bowl upon the top of it, and his seven lamps thereon, and seven pipes to the seven lamps, which are upon the top thereof'" (Zechariah 4:1-2, KJV).

Zechariah's vision was before Christ, so it lacked the details that John, who was after Christ, could give. John in his vision points out who or what the candlestick represents. This mystery of the seven lamps was explained in chapter 1 of the book of Revelation. "And I turned to see the voice that spake with me. And being turned, I saw seven golden candlesticks; And in the midst of the seven candlesticks, one like unto the Son of man, clothed with a garment down to the foot, and girt about the paps [waistline] with a golden girdle. His head and his hairs were white as white as snow; and his eyes were as a flame of fire; And his feet like unto fine brass, as if they burned in a furnace; and his voice as the sound of many waters, And he had in his right hand seven stars: and out of his mouth went a sharp two-edged sword: and his countenance was as the sun shineth in his strength. And when I saw him, I fell at his feet as dead. And he laid his right hand upon me, saying unto me, Fear not; I am the first and the last: I am he that liveth, and was dead; and, behold, I am alive for evermore, Amen; and have the keys of hell and of death. (Revelation 1:12-18, KJV)

John saw the Christ in his gloried state. Yet what he saw was a symbol, or image of a prophetic message written in a mysterious language subject to interpretation. A brief interpretation of the image of the man John saw reveals the image of the Son of God whose words are truth (sharp two-edged sword), his wisdom unfathomable (hair white as snow), and his eyes as a flame of fire (showing in him the Spirit of God, the light and the fire of the Spirit of the Father). His body is seen as fully clothed in righteousness (no impurity in him). The color of his feet represents the mixing of people of all races, and nations, that will stand as one man in the earth. These were tried, made holy, and found worthy to be part of His glorious body. This is the new man that God is creating in the earth, who inhabits the fullness of God. The stars in the hands of the man John saw were the angels of the seven churches. This we know from the one who was speaking to John: "Write the things which thou hast seen, and the things which are, and the things which shall be hereafter; the mystery of the seven stars which thou sawest in my right hand, and the seven golden candlesticks. The seven stars are the angels of the seven churches: and the seven candlesticks, which thou sawest, are the seven churches" (Revelation 1:19-20, KJV).

The seven stars are the seven lamps that Zechariah saw and the seven pipes are the seven churches. The vision of Zechariah was incomplete, in that John saw the Lord in the midst of the candlesticks.

However, the prophet Zechariah also saw Christ as the stone, or the man whom John saw walking in the midst of the candlesticks. Zechariah wrote, "For behold the stone that I have laid before Joshua; upon one stone shall be seven eyes . . . For who hath despised the day of small things? For they shall rejoice, and shall see the plummet in the hand of Zerrubbabel with those seven; they are the eyes of the Lord, which run to and fro through the earth" (Zechariah 3:9; 4:10, KJV). Those are the seven Spirits of God that go to and fro throughout the earth beholding the good and the evil to give to everyman his just reward.

That we know from the book of Revelation where we read, "And unto the angel of the church in Sardis write; These things saith he that hath the seven Spirits of God, and the seven stars . . . And I beheld, and, lo, in the midst of the throne and of the four beasts, and in the midst of the elders, stood a lamb as it had been slain, having seven horns and seven eyes, which are the seven Spirits of God" (Revelation 3:1; 5:6, KJV). The angels of the churches and the Spirits of God that are assigned to the seven churches, with Christ in the center, are the fulfillment the mystery of God, and the power of His Christ. The chart below shows the relationship between the various symbols.

Symbols Chart		
Lamps	=	Stars
Stone	=	Lamb
7 Spirits of God	=	7 Eyes
4 Horses	=	4 Manifestations of Spirits
Bow	=	Instruments of War
Rider	=	Righteousness (God's Word & Spirit)
Crown	=	First Nation
Golden Candlesticks	=	7 Churches
7 Stars	=	Angels of the 7 churches

There are other details about one symbol briefly described earlier, the "rider on the white horse," that must be explored further. In the book of Revelation, the white horse equates to one of the four spirits that God will send on the earth that the prophet speaks of in the book of Zechariah (Zechariah 6:2-5, KJV). The rider on the white horse had a crown on his head. This crown is representative of the first nation that God will use to go forth to conquer on His behalf. Later chapters in this work will provide more information on this conquering nation. The rider held a bow that represents the instruments of war (Genesis 48: 22, KJV).

The horse is symbolic of a spirit of righteousness that God will send forth throughout the world calling nations to the obedience of faith. I saw in a vision the horse and the rider. They were both spirits. These spirits come from heaven and inhabit the bodies of men and nations.

> Behold, there came four chariots out from between two mountains . . . In the first chariot were red horses; and in the second chariot black horses; And in the third chariot white horses; and in the fourth chariot grizzled and bay horses. Then I answered and said unto the angel that talked with me, "What are these, my Lord?" And the angel answered and said unto me, "These are the four spirits of heaven, which go forth from standing before the Lord of all the earth." (Zechariah 6:1-5, KJV)

The four spirits represent the first four seals spoken of in the book of Revelation. Each seal or horse represents a spirit that will be sent into the earth.

The above-referenced symbols strictly deal with images described in the opening of the first seal. The following chapters describe the nations and peoples that are also a part of the first seal. Furthermore, the information in the following chapters will detail their identities and roles in the fulfillment of the events of the first seal.

Comparison Charts

Prophetic Comparisons of Daniel and other prophets including John's Revelations	
Daniel	John
Daniel 7:4 The First Beast (like a lion)	Revelation 6:1-2 The White Horse
Daniel 7:5 The Second Beast (like a bear)	Revelation 6:4 The Red Horse
Daniel 7:6 The Third Beast (like a leopard)	Revelation 6:5 The Black Horse
Daniel 7:7 The Fourth Beast (dreadful and terrible with iron teeth and ten horns)	Revelation 6:8a The Pale Horse
Daniel 7:8 The Fifth Beast (little horn)	Revelation 6:8b Hell follows

Daniel 7: Four Beasts	Ezekiel 37: Dry Bones	Personal Visions	Zachariah 6: Four Chariots	Revelation 6: Seven Seals
The First Beast (like a lion with eagles wings hearth like a man)		United States Africa western Europe Christians		White Horse Rider, bow and crowns, conquering to conquer

Symbols of Nations	Location of People in the world	Seal
Black	North	Third
dappled	South	Fourth
white	North	First
Red	Throughout earth	Second

Symbols of Nations	Symbols of People	Timeline
Horns	Sea /water	
Beast	Sheep/cows	
Humans	Male/female	

The Nations and People of the First Seal

In an effort to clarify the identity and purpose of the first nation and its people that are a part of the first seal, we must extract the information embedded in the dreams of the prophet Daniel. Daniel's writing about his dreams discusses four beasts. The four beasts are directly representative of the nations that will come to power and dominate the events described in the first four seals mentioned in the book of Revelation, as well as the four groups of horses mentioned by the prophet Zechariah.

In this section, we will only deal with the first beast and its relationship to the first seal. When the prophecies of Daniel, Zechariah, and John, as well as my personal revelations as listed in the chart above, are put together, the identities of the nations and their role in end-time prophecy will be clearly revealed. We will be reading about nations, spiritual and natural identities, people that are inhabited by spirits, some good and some bad, and forces that control man and his destiny.

Daniel's Four Beasts

God has left us with prophetic blueprints to follow and use as guides to understand His word. As He said in Hosea, "I have spoken by the prophets, and I have multiplied visions, and used similitude, by the ministry of the prophets" (Hos. 12:10). We can follow what will take place from toward the end of Daniel's dreams as we compare them to Nebuchadnezzar's dreams. The significance of Daniel's dream and visions are that they are not a repeat of Nebuchadnezzar's, but a prophetic blueprint and continuance of Nebuchadnezzar's dream,

The stone that struck the feet of Nebuchadnezzar's image has grown and will grow into a great mountain. Yet we will see a similarity at the end of this age where the stone will again strike the ten nations that will arise. The epic struggle will now conclude with this generation playing a role in the fulfillment of the prophecy. We already showed how Nebuchadnezzar's image was fulfilled. Now Daniel's dreams must also happen. The union of people and nations, and the universe engaged in the war for dominion, will be a great occurrence, and the world will be invited to attend. Some will be a part of it on the side of good, and others will be clueless as to what is taking place around them, and some will join the side of evil.

In the first year of Belshazzar king of Babylon, Daniel had a dream and visions of his head upon his bed, concerning the things that were to come upon the earth: Daniel wrote, "I saw in my visions by night, and

behold, the four winds of the heaven strove upon the great sea. And four
great beasts came up from the sea, diverse one from another. The first
was like a lion and had eagle's wings:

"I beheld until the wing thereof was plucked, and it was lifted
up from the earth, and made to stand upon the feet as a man,
and a man's heart was given to it." (Daniel 7:1-4, KJV)

The coming forth of this first beast is the beginning of the seventy-year
period and the opening of the first seal. Daniel said of those beasts;
"These great beasts, which are four, are four kings that shall arise out of
the earth" (Daniel 7:17, KJV). These correspond to Nebuchadnezzar's
great image, which is a prophetic similitude of the nations that will arise
to power. Earlier, we read the interpretation that the horses represent
spirits that God would send into the earth. The beasts of Daniel's dreams
will come forth with a particular type of spirit. Zechariah points this out
in his writing about four chariots:

And again I looked up and saw four chariots coming out from
between two mountains and the mountains were mountains of
brass. In the first chariot were red horses; and in the second
chariot black horses; and in the third chariot white horses; and
in the fourth chariot grizzled and bay horses. Then I answered
and said unto the angel that talked with me, "What are these,
my Lord?" And the angel answered and said unto me, "These

are the four spirits of the heavens, which go forth from standing
before the Lord of all the earth." (Zechariah 6:1-5, KJV)

These spirits represent the spirits behind the nations and the events
that are coming upon the earth. The rest of this chapter relates to the
first beast, the nation of the first seal, its rise and fall, and the names
that God revealed to me that identifies it to this generation. The first
kingdom will go through a spiritual transformation or a divinely inspired
revolution.

The rider on the white horse had a crown on his head. This crown
represents the first group of nations that God will use to go forth to
conquer on His behalf. The rider also held a bow, which represents the
instruments of war (Gen. 48:22), and the type of war is stated clearly that
he went forth in righteousness conquering and to conquer.

The other horses went into different parts of the earth as the prophet
wrote, the black horses went toward the north, the white toward the
west, the dappled went toward the south and the red went throughout
the earth. Each of these groups of spirits will be studied individually, but
for now, we will follow them as they go into the country to which they
are sent. When the sprits go forth, they bring with them a particular
atmosphere that transforms the people and the environment. Prophecy
is sure because the heavens rule and God releases the spirits that will
fulfill his word on the earth. God declares the beginning from the end
and sends his prophets with the revelations.

CHAPTER NINE

Two Nations

Throughout the dreams and visions, which I received, there was always one thing that remained constant. Two women I saw with child, two kingdoms I saw arose, two prophets, two rulers, and two sets of people. Yet these are formed in the womb of one mother. These two kingdoms and people were mentioned throughout the prophesies. These two always eventually joined together to become one. Beginning with the prophet Ezekiel who said, "Son of man, there were two women, the daughters of one mother: And they committed whoredoms in Egypt; they committed whoredoms in their youth: there they bruised the teats of their virginity. And the names of them were Aholah, the elder, and Aholibah her sister: and they were mine, and they bear sons and daughters. Thus were their names; Samaria is Aholah, and Jerusalem Aholibah" (Ezek. 23:2-4).

Those scriptures reference the children of Israel who are circumcised in the flesh. However, there are a group of children through Jesus Christ who are circumcised in the heart and filled with the Holy Ghost. These belong to the free woman or Jerusalem who is above and the Mother of those born of the Spirit and save by grace. (See Galatians 4.) These are the members of Christ's body that make up the bride of the Lord Jesus.

The focus at this time will be on the people of the Church that God purchased with his own blood. The members are scattered through out the world, and God will gather them into one body.

The other groups of people are the Jews who have been blinded until the appointed time. The apostle Paul said that God will save them with the same grace with which God saved the church. For there will come a time when all Israel will be saved. Micah prophesied concerning them, "Therefore will he give them up, until the time that, she which travailed hath brought forth: then the remnant of his brethren shall return unto the children of Israel." The Apostle Paul also wrote, "For I would not brethren that ye should be ignorant of this mystery, lest ye should be wise in your own conceit, that blindness in parties happened to Israel, until the fullness of the Gentiles be come in. And so all Israel will be saved, as is written, 'there shall come out of Zion the Deliverer, and shall turn away ungodliness from Jacob: For this is my covenant with them when I shall take away their sins.' As concerning the gospel, they are enemies for your sakes: but as touching the election, they are beloved for the fathers' sake" (Rom 11:25-28).

The promises that God made to Abraham to be a father of many nations and the promises he made to Isaac and Jacob will be fulfilled through this group of people, "for salvation is of the Jews." God will graph them back into the tree that they were broken off from. I will be writing about what God gave me about them, but now I will focus on the people of the church.

Dream One

Concerning these things, this was revealed to me. In one dream, I saw standing on a street corner, under a light from a light pole, surrounded by the darkness of the night, a man, as if waiting. Then there came to him a white horse that began speaking to him. After speaking to him, it started walking on a road that led up hill, darkened by the night. He followed the horse up the dark hill, and it led him to a well-lit building. As he entered the building, he saw two women in the early stages of pregnancy. One was further along than the other. The women were preparing for a great feast.

These two women represent the two families of Rachel (Joseph) and Leah (Judah) who built the house of Israel as said in the scripture, "The Lord make the woman that is come into thine house like Rachel and like Leah, which two did build the house of Israel" (Ruth 4:11). These two groups of people will be gathered under one king. The prophet Micah also wrote, "The Lord will assemble her that halteth, and will gather her that is driven out, and her that He afflicted. And I will make her that halteth a remnant, and her that was cast far off a strong nation: and the Lord shall reign over them in mount Zion (Mic.4:6-7). Here again, two different women bring forth children, each having a unique place and role in scripture and prophecy.

The women also represent the religious bodies that God uses to bring forth spiritual life. The Christian Church and the sanctified, born again Jews, gathered out of the nations and the land of Israel. that will bring forth two nations of people that will be birthed in the earth. These two bodies will eventually become one kingdom, having over them one Shepherd, one Lord, and Savior over all, and in them all.

Dream Two

I saw in another dream two men whom God will use to gather Israel back to Him in one body. These two men will unify the people of and the nations of God. Through these two men and the groups of people, Christians and Jews, God will subdue the earth in righteousness. In the dream, I saw how the two anointed men were climbing a mountain on opposite sides, one on the east, the other on the west. They both reached the top at approximately the same time. However, the one from the west came up first.

As they reached the top, I saw nothing but darkness. After a period of gross darkness, I heard a voice saying, "I see blood." Then I saw blood on the mountain, and then I saw the mountain filled with light.

Before going into the interpretation of the dream, I need to mention that in another dream, I saw two Hebrew men identified to me as two prophets. Those two men it was revealed to me, are the prophets that John wrote about in the book of Revelation. "These are the two olive trees and the two candlesticks standing before the God of the earth" (Rev.11:4). I will write about those two in another book, but I mentioned them now to avoid any confusion with the other two men whom I saw climbing the mountain. When we read the symbols that the prophet Zechariah wrote about to describe those two prophets, there is a very interesting part to the symbol that describes the two other men about whom we are going to read.

The prophet was talking with an angel, and he enquired about the candlestick and the olive trees. The angel explained to him the meaning of the candlesticks, along with their seven lamps. He stated that they represented Zerrubbabel with the seven eyes of the lord which run to and fro throughout the earth. Zerubbabel through the Spirit of God will build the house of God, bringing forth the headstone, "Crying Grace grace unto it." When John saw the Lord in the book of Revelation he also had with him the seven Spirits of God, as He stood in the midst of the golden candlestick. This symbolic man will bring down the great nations of the world by the power of the Spirit of God.

Then he asked, "What are these two olive trees upon the right side of the candlestick and upon the left side thereof? And I answered again and said unto him, "What be these two olive branches which through the two golden pipes empty the golden oil out of themselves." The angel answered him, "These are the two anointed ones that stands before the Lord of the whole earth" (Zech. 4:11-14).

Here we come to a very interesting part of the prophecy.

The two olive branches through which the golden oil flows are two Christian men through whom the Lord will pour out His Spirit upon the earth. These are the branches that are grafted into the olive tree. These are the men referred to as the branch whom I saw climbing the mountain on opposite sides. These two anointed men will complete the building of the house of the Lord. As we read further, their work and the revelations about how they impact the Gentile world, will become clear to the reader. These two figures are prophetic links that clarify the missing links in prophetic evolution. There is much written about the last days, with emphasis on the last seven years. These two men and their respective ministry tie us into the last days, with emphasis on the last seventy years

The interpretation of the dream is that the Lord will raise up rulers in the church. One will be raised up in the west, and one in the east. One will be a prophet and the other a king/prophet. Each will be building and promoting the kingdom of God and promoting the gospel through the means appointed to them by God and will be involved in a bloody period when darkness seeks to cover the earth. There will be much spilling of blood during the period of darkness.

The mountain represents the nations of the world on the east and the west, that will be converted to Christ and form the kingdom of God in the earth. The blood after the period of darkness refers to the Great War that will follow some evil days on the earth. This will be a time when evil will seek to rule over the earth. During that period, the world will go through World War Three, and some difficult times, filled with darkness and much shedding of blood. The time of light that follows, will be a time when the whole world will be filled with the knowledge of God, and these men empty the golden oil out of themselves.

These men are referred to as the branch because as Paul so eloquently illustrated, Israel is the olive tree that bears the root. The Gentiles are the branches that are grafted in. These two Christian rulers will be used by God to build the church into a dominant power in the earth as they prepare the members for the return of the Lord Jesus. One of the men will be a prophet in the west whom the Lord will use to gather the church into one body. The other will be an emperor and prophet whom the Lord will use to gather nations unto him. He will rise to power through wars and be a skillful and wise ruler.

The Branches

The Lord showed me the prophet who will arise in the west standing on a limb that extended out prominently from a tree. He was standing in the light of God on the branch. He is one of the two anointed men spoken of in the book of Zechariah. The angel told Joshua, the crown high priest, that God was going to bring forth his servant, The Branch. The branches through the grace of God will unify the body, and in the end, every man will call his neighbor under the vine and under the fig tree (Zech. 3: 8-10).

The prophet Jeremiah also wrote about one of the men called the "Branch." "Behold the days will come, saith the Lord, that I will raise unto David a righteous Branch, and a king shall reign and prosper, and shall execute judgment and justice in the earth. In his days, Judah shall be saved, and Israel shall dwell safely, and this is the name whereby he shall be called, THE LORD OUR RIGHTEOUSNESS. Therefore, behold, the days come, saith the Lord, that they shall no more say, The Lord liveth, which brought up and which the seed of the house of Israel out of the North country, and from all countries whither I had driven them; and they shall dwell in their own land" (Jer. 23:5-8). Jeremiah goes into a little detail about what the branch will accomplish during the time of his ministry. The prophet Isaiah also wrote extensively of the servants of the Lord, describing in detail their works. One of the things they will accomplish in the earth will be to magnify the law and glorify God. They will gather the people of God and turn their hearts to the true and living God, to serve him without fear.

Revelations about the Two

These are the two rulers over the people of God who will bring us to the end. They are sent to prepare the world to meet its maker. The two rulers who will lead the families of God will do exploits during the time of their respective coming forth. The Psalmist prophesied that the people will be willing in the day of their power. At the end of the period of darkness, the manifestation of the power of God will be global. I saw how the two men were lifted up from the earth and exalted very high. These two anointed men will not only proclaim the gospel, but during their time, I saw a great outpouring of the Spirit of God after the man on the eastern side of the mountain came out of the darkness. It filled the earth with the Spirit, glory, and knowledge of God. I also saw the messenger from the west pouring out oil in the west. After the outpouring of the oil, the people were filled with the Holy Ghost. The outpouring of the Holy Spirit will begin in the west, then after there will be the great outpouring in the east and the north and south. The whole world will be filled with the glory and the knowledge of the Lord.

In a related dream, I saw the messenger from the west standing in an open field during the night. The only light was that of the moon, which shone around him. In the open field, he was waving a white flag as if calling the nations in the west to righteousness. Then from heaven, I saw sprinkling the earth, as it appeared to me, balls of light. This was different from the king in the east, who, as I saw, in his day will baptize people with the Holy Ghost and fire. His coming forth will be as the brightness of the sunrise. When he arises, those in the west will know, for his glory as was shown to me will be as the rising sun whose rays reached the west. Likewise, when the prophet in the west arises, one of his journeys will be to Africa to teach and preach the gospel. Those in the east will know, for they shall see the wisdom of God in him.

Finally, I saw the prophet from the west riding a white horse. Great light surrounded the horse and rider, but it was a short ride on a narrow path. The interpretation is that the Lord will perform a quick work during those days. In another dream, I saw the ruler from the east, riding the white horse. The two riders represent the two men and the two sets of children whom they are gathering together by the Spirit of God. These two sets of children are from one father and mother. They make up the body of Christ in the earth. Male and female God created man. This is true also for the second Adam, who is a quickening Spirit. These two will rule the nations of the earth with a rod of iron and through the power of God.

With the opening of the first seal, the writer from the book of Revelation said he saw a rider on a white horse going forth conquering and to conquer. The rider/s on the white horse corresponds to the first beast that Daniel saw. The beast was like a lion and had eagle's wings. Daniel said, "I beheld till the wings thereof were plucked, and it was lifted up from the earth, and made to stand upon the feet as a man, and a man's heart was given to it" (Dan.7:4). The beast must be changed, humbled, and then raised to glory. Let us read from the prophets how this will happen. First, we must identify the nations whose wings will be plucked and the one having the body of a lion that will go forth conquering and to conquer.

CHAPTER TEN

Daniel's Beast Identified

Before we identify the nations and the people associated with the beast, there are other dreams and visions that I must share that relate to Daniel's dream. In one dream, I saw two separate groups of animals, a herd of cattle and a small group of sheep. The cattle were of mixed colors, black and white. A man tended the sheep that were white, and the large numbers of cattle were tended by the man from the west. He was leading the cattle through a field. After the herd passed through the field, the sheep that were standing apart followed in the track of the cattle.

After the sheep passed through the field, I saw a huge lion that came out of the direction the sheep came, and he followed the sheep.

These are three groups of people, one representing the house of Judah: the lion part of the body, another, the house of Joseph, represented in the west, and the small group, the remnant of Israel at Palestine. The cattle of different colors are the eagle part of the body. (See Ezekiel 34:17, 31.) Remember Joseph had the coat of many colors and to his sons were given the blessings of prosperity. This is reflected in the world, which has been blessed with material prosperity, so much so that it runs over the walls, but especially the United States. These nations will God raise up as the tabernacle of Joseph.

The House of Judah and Joseph

The scripture says, "There shall come a star out of Jacob, and a scepter shall rise out of Israel. There will be two nations of God, Israel and Judah, and out of Israel shall come he that shall have dominion, as was prophesied by Balaam" (Num.24:17, 19.). When these two nations of people arise in their fullness, the whole earth will be filled with God's glory. For the prophet Isaiah said, "He shall cause them that came out of

Jacob to take root: Israel shall blossom and bud, and fill the face of the world with fruit" (Is. 27:6).

Finally, I saw the man that went into the waters clothed with the woman from heaven, walk out of the deep waters unto the shores, and stand upon the sand of the shore. As he stood there, the ruler from the east who always had a multitude following him, every time I saw him in a dream or vision, also came out of the waters unto the shores. However, he was on the opposite side of the one from the west. These two stood out of the waters in that order and will come forth in that order.

Those two men represent two kingdoms, two groups of religious people, and literally two men. These will be filled with the Spirit of God and with power. The nation of Israel represents the group of sheep that I saw. A high priest from the tribe of Levi will arise in Israel who will minister the truth and teach and preach salvation to the Jews through a right understanding of the law. There will always be a remnant in Israel who will follow and accept Jesus as Lord. God has not forsaken nor ever will forsake the Jews, but will continue to use them to fulfill his divine purpose.

The lion represents an African emperor and Christian Africa, and the cattle being guided by the man from the west, represents the Christian people from the west. The kingdom of God will come with mighty signs and wonders by the power of the Spirit of God, and filled with true holiness, justice, and righteousness. As it is written, "For our gospel came not unto you in word only, but also in power, and in the Holy Ghost, and in much assurance . . . And ye became followers of us, and of the Lord, having received the word in much affliction, with joy of the Holy Ghost" (1 Thess. 1:5-6). Those who are born of water and the Spirit are the children of God.

Daniel's beast represents those nations of people filled with the Spirit of God. Christians are a people meek as a lamb and harmless as doves, filled with good works, but also wise as serpents because their wisdom is from God. These will be protected by the greatest armies on the earth. One will rule the skies as the eagle, and the other, the land like the lion. The United States of America leading the western world, and the United Christian States of Africa, along with the state of Israel, leading the continent of Africa and parts of the Middle East, make up Daniel's first beast. Yes, Africa will be transformed into a mighty and powerful union. It was described to me as a lion with an army that will be as fierce as killer bees. The ruler will rule with a rod of iron. Israel will also have a remnant, which will follow the lamb and be protected by the west and the south.

It should be noted that those from the west have with them all the power and glory of the most powerful nations on earth backing them. The United States will be exalted in glory and power and will be a champion around the world for justice in the earth. Israel, though small, will be a force to reckon with in technology, science, and military power. Together these kingdoms will magnify the law of God on earth while showing forth his glory and praises. The beast that Daniel saw being lifted up from the earth corresponds to John's vision of the woman bringing forth her Son.

Another prophecy concerning these two people forming into one, was mentioned by Jesus who said, "And other sheep I have, which are not of this fold: them also I must bring and they shall hear my voice; and there shall be one fold, and one shepherd" (John 10:16). So when Jesus, who came as a Jew, said to the woman at the well, "Ye worship ye know not what: we know what we worship; for salvation is of the Jews;" he was speaking of then and now.

These two nations God will use to show forth his glory. The prophet, foreseeing this, wrote, "The envy also of Ephraim shall depart, and the adversaries of Judah shall be cut off: Ephraim shall not envy Judah, and Judah shall not vex Ephraim. But they shall fly upon the shoulders of the Philistine toward the west; they shall spoil them of the east together: they shall lay their hand upon Edom and Moab; and the children of Ammon shall obey them" (Isa.11:9-14). Here again we see the two families that God will raise up in the earth, Judah and Ephraim, the two families that God refers to throughout the scriptures that will bring salvation to the world.

MESSAGE TO THE CHURCH

Christiansted, St. Croix, V.I. 00820
778-6311 Ext. 2154 or 2197
July 23, 1992

Reverend George
Christiansted.
St. Croix, V.I. 00822

Dear Reverend:

Greetings in the holy name of Jesus Christ our Lord the true immortal potentate, King of Kings and Lord of Lords. Peace be with you and your household.

In response to our telephone conversation, I am writing to you this letter. The Lord has given me a word for the church, and being of like faith and common belief, I felt it only proper to relate to you first (The Ministerial Association) what has been given to me for the church.

There are many concerns that need to be addressed and so it is necessary to sit with you face to face and share the information I have received from the Lord, and likewise receive from you whatever instructions you may have received from the Lord.

My brothers, the time is short, and much work needs to be done. There is a set time that we have to work with, so the need to get this message to you and for us to formulate a working agenda is of paramount importance. I will be looking forward to hearing from you as to when and where we can meet.

You can contact me via Sister V. whom you know is like a mother to me, and truly my mother in faith, or you can reach me at the address or phone number listed above.

My brothers, let us be prayerful as we continue to shepherd the Lord's flock through the times that are ahead of us. The grace of our Lord and Savior Jesus Christ be with you, and may his love sustain you.

Your Fellow Servant,
Austin Phillips

August 8, 1992
Pastors and Ministers of the Gospel
St. Croix, U.S. Virgin Islands

Greetings in the name of Jesus the Son of God; God the Father, God the Holy Ghost our eternal peace, comfort and rest.

May the rich blessings of wisdom and understanding overflow in you, and may the Holy Spirit of truth guide you in all the truth concerning the mysteries of God, that He has chosen at this time to reveal to you. Having much things to say to you, which I 'have received from the Lord, and desirous to participate in your efforts to bring glory to the Most High God, by standing up against those forces that are destructive to the communities. I'm now writing to you in hope to impart that which God has given to me, to you.

How can it be, that this place, a fruitful land inhabited by a majority of Christians, be plagued with so much evil? My brethren, the Father has chosen to give this land to us to show forth His glory. That which has been preordained, as spoken of by the Prophets, is about to be fulfilled in this generation; where the Church of the Living God will be an example of righteousness to the nations of the world.

Though the giants will be there to hinder, the Word of God to you is a sure Word. Righteousness and Justice must go forth from this nation, and our generation has been blessed to do it. There is much work to be done: The restoration of the family, the re-gathering of the dispersed flocks, and the unification of the saints to the glory of the body.

Holy brethren the right to subdue devils, and to bring to nought principalities and powers, was given to the Church. The Lord has chosen this generation of saints to exercise great power on the earth, that His faithfulness and righteousness will be plainly manifested for all to see.

The responsibility of the pastors, and all those who handle the Word of God is a noble calling, and should not be taken lightly in this generation of evil and perversity. To live among ourselves in the way presented by Christ; a Holy Nation, a Royal Priesthood, a people called to exalt the name of Jesus, is a privilege that we can exercise here in this country.

Beloved, we must note the time that we are living in. Therefore, consider prayerfully the reason for my request to talk to you face to face and share with you that which the Lord has given to me.

These words are true and faithful and may our God speedily perform them for the time is at hand. I, Austin, salute you in Jesus Holy Name, and may His Spirit of Grace, Love and Peace sustain us now and forever more.

Some of the issues that I want to discuss include:

1. Addressing the alarming drug problem of St. Croix. This problem can be confronted by the Church more effectively, not just through prayer and treatment centers, but by us going into the neighborhoods in masse. In going into these neighborhoods in masse, we can spend a week or two at the site where drugs are openly sold, and minister to that community. We can demonstrate with placards and signs, and work with that community to take back their streets from the drug dealers. We can help to establish a crime watch in those areas that have a high incidence of crime and violence. WE can free the community from the spirits that now have men bound.

2. Help in the physical restoration of run-down dirty neighborhoods, by actively working with its members to clean up those neighborhoods (many hands make work easy).

    Help provide a quality life for the poor and needy, because we are Christians.

3. The time is coming where the church will have to do more than provide inspiration and counseling to its members. The physical needs of its members will also have to be addressed. To prepare for such a time, the church need to develop agricultural and economic programs, that will make it self sufficient in providing the basic needs, of its members.

Along with addressing physical concerns, the need for ministers to establish an effective church community where all churches and all members are one, in unity with the Church, so that a disciplinary action by one denomination is carried out throughout the various sects. In other words, should an individual violate a commandment and is placed in suspension, the suspension of that person should be enforceable no matter where that individual goes. Also that sin would be discouraged in the church community. I must point towards the need for the church to begin to operate as a nation within a nation, and be the moral conscience, the light, in the community in which we live. We must also remember the instructions of the apostle Paul to Timothy, to instruct the rich to do good, to be rich in good works to be generous and ready to share (1 Tim. 6:18). In Titus we find, the instructions for all the believers; For Jesus, "Gave Himself for us, that He might redeem us from every lawless deed and purify for Himself, a people for His own possession, zealous for good deeds" (Titus 2:14).

So then let us go forth conquering and to conquer and bring an end through divine right, authority and power to this present system of evil, and wickedness. This is the Word of the Lord to you, oh Saints, the true ambassadors for peace and those who carry the gospel of Salvation to a hungry world. In coming together, we will show how hate has no place in a civilized world.

These are just a few concerns that I want to discuss with you, as we work together toward the salvation of St. Croix. Remember, faith without works is dead, and no one is justified by faith alone (James 2:24).

Brother Austin Phillips
General Delivery Christiansted, St. Croix U.S. Virgin Islands 00820

Brother Austin Phillips
General Delivery Christiansted, St. Croix U.S. Virgin Islands 00820

Pastors/Ministers April 9, 1993
Holy Brethren,

Greetings in the name of Jesus the Son of God, God the Father, and God the Holy Ghost, our eternal peace, comfort, and rest.

This second time I am writing to you, so as to give these words as I have received them. I pray that we meditate soberly on them, and that we all come to a common understanding, as to the work that God is now calling us to do. When I first wrote to you, my plea was that the saints join together to confront and address the many social problems that are now flourishing in our communities. I pointed out to you that unity is a prerequisite for God to use us as a body for him to be glorified through. The Lord will not repent from this call to this generation to show forth His glory, and this nation to be the executor of true justice, and its citizens examples of righteousness. It is not the Father's desire that the wicked rule over the righteous nor for poverty and oppression to be the bread of the poor.

Brethren, we are called to right many wrongs, and to give the weak and lowly a living hope and the assurance of justice and peace. We cannot ignore this call of God, nor can we afford to turn away from the cries of the multitude of sufferers, for it is obvious the cries will only grow louder, and that if left alone the wicked will spread themselves to cover the land. Today God is calling us to stand as one man, and to work toward the building up of His church nation, so that His name would be highly exalted in the earth. We have been chosen to be the instruments of His righteousness, this land being one of the places from where He will execute justice in the earth.

Let us then go forward with the full understanding that we are to lead a generation of people to God, a people who is to be born in this wilderness of darkness and sin. This people God has chosen to use to glorify himself through and to show the world how men ought to live. So you ministers are now charged with a double responsibility. First the building up of His Kingdom, starting with His Holy nation here on St. Croix, and that being the force to revolutionize the rest of the United States of America into a holy spiritual Kingdom on the earth. Again I reiterate, justice and truth must proceed from America, and we are the generation that the Lord is calling upon to shout as the angels "Glory to God in the Highest and on earth peace among men with whom He is pleased." The world is calling out for peace and justice, and daily the spread of global conflict brings home more clearly the perilous times with which we are faced. I saw a body of evil spirits spreading across the country, until the Spirit of the Lord, drove it back (to its place of origin), and then completely off the land. God has left us with a hope, and is pointing us to a way of escape from the evil that has been set loose upon the earth; giving the assurance of victory through Him.

Holy Brethren, I long to see the day when glory and praise will be upon the lips of all the inhabitants of the land because of what God intends to do with this land, through His church the rightful inhabitants of this land. The fruits of our labors today toward the glorification of God, and His Kingdom will yield fruits of quietness and assurance for our generation and the ones after us. We the saints must arm ourselves with all the armaments of God, and begin first in the kingdom of God to battle against those forces of divisionism, and lawlessness, breaking down those denominational barriers that weaken such a mighty people, and subject us to live far below the standard of glory that God, from the beginning, had ordained for us.

Let me encourage you Brethren to communicate often with one another, not just with the minister that you know and work with, but with all the faithful brethren. Let us come to know one another and encourage one another in every good work, Praying that God will link our spirits together with cords of love. I must also point out the need for praying and fasting together as a ministerial group, and to encourage praying and fasting together amongst the congregation. The people must be prepared with one mind to receive the Spirit from on high who will empower us to accomplish this great work that is ahead of us. For we must know these simple requirements will bring great results, for it is not by power, or by the might of man that the Lord will glorify Himself, but by the Spirit which will not only bring glory to God, but to the entire body.

I trust everyone will examine his gifts and calling, and give faithfully of that which they have received to the building up of the Kingdom. We must teach our members how to respect and honor ministry, so that they may know how to receive a minister of God, for a minister is a minister to the whole Kingdom, and should be honored as such. Brethren we need to practice speaking a common language. I would suggest reading together as a body of ministers, on a regular schedule, sharing the truth as God gave it and praying that the Spirit of Wisdom and revelation would manifest in our midst to give us a common understanding. Any difficult questions that need to be answered, the Lord will reveal to us as long as we come together with an open mind to receive of God's word. Also as ministers we must show ourselves to be faithful, and courageous, so as to encourage the saints who look to us as examples; giving them the confidence in the victory of the church over the forces of hell. Remember we did not receive a spirit of fear, but of power and love, and of a sound mind, as well as weapons that are mighty through God, to the pulling down of strongholds.

When we as ministers can show a perfect unity amongst ourselves, others of the faith and even those not of the faith, will happily want to join themselves to the church, for this unity will have the sure promise of glory. God will bless us. Let us love one another. There is a real need to remind you of the social conditions of the community and of the growing sentiments of resentment and mistrust between the various ethnic and religious groups. The spirits of hate, cruelty and greed have gone forth again into the world. Racism, fascism, humanism and perversion are growing and we must not neglect to discuss these issues amongst ourselves, and devise spiritual strategies to keep them from spreading, and devouring our communities. The need for a church nation, filled with power from on high to effectively combat the evils that are plaguing our communities will be welcomed by the multitude who hunger and thirst after truth and justice. Let me remind you that all power and authority in heaven and on earth was given to the church, including the right to subdue nations to the authority of God.

The will of God is to save the United States, and He has shown me that the very government will change, and will be changed by the Christian believers in the country who will abhor the degenerate and immoral condition of the government. The United States is to be a representative of God's glory, and a country to whom the world is to look toward for guidance and instruction in justice. This is a country rich in resources, and its military might is unquestionable. However, today because of the evils of the government, these resources and the military might is being used for evil more than for the good of the country. God is going to turn that around through us, His body. He will use the precious lives and resources of this country for good, and not as it is this day, for evil. The majority of the inhabitants of this land hold to a similar Christian faith, so the country is sometimes referred to as a Christian country to the shame of Christianity.

This country today is too immoral and unjust to be called a Christian nation, but that is because the church sits in the shadow of this vile government as a scattered people, robbed by many who use God's name for their own personal gain, thus causing disunity and shame in the Kingdom. Brethren this country is under a direct assault from God. Natural disasters will increase as well as poverty, lawlessness, and military losses. International prestige and influence will diminish. Violent crimes and hatred between the races will grow, and the economic miracle that the president is now proposing will prove to be an economic nightmare. God will not honor the wicked, and for the saints not to make a distinction between that which is good and that which is evil is an error which will bring more judgment upon the land. For God will destroy the wicked from the land, and He has called this generation to show forth His righteousness; let us not neglect such a great calling. "Righteousness exalts a nation, and sin is a reproach to any people." Likewise, "the nation that forgets God will be turned into hell." We brethren are called to save the country.

The Lord is already preparing the people's hearts to receive His salvation, but we must first correct our deficiencies and clean up our act, in order for us to be the head of this nation, and not as we are this day, a weak, divided, and scattered community. Every generation of decline shows more the weakness of the church, for the state and health of the church is reflected in the state and health of the community. The church must be united, and nationally organized in order to combat and eradicate the forces of evil that break down the community and destroy lives. To do otherwise would be to sacrifice the next generation to devils and demons.

During the years of judgment as the Lord calls the nation to repentance, the degree of lawlessness and violence will be multiplied to frightening heights. The policies and actions of this government will miserably fail, and the honor and dignity of the proud Americans will be reduced to nothing. It is a people such as this that the Lord will call, and they will answer. How will He call them except through us the lights of His Kingdom. "Come unto me all ye that labor and are heavy laden, and ye shall find rest for your soul, for my yoke is easy and my burden is light." This should be the motto of the church, who was given all power and authority in heaven and on earth to bind and lose, to heal and to build up, to comfort and restore the broken hearted and satisfy the hungry souls. First we must address the important task of establishing the perfect model of justice and uprightness in the church nation, where morality and holiness is a badge of honor. This is the church's' true calling in America. This is its destiny.

When we are in harmony with the word and will of God we can call the country to repentance with a unified voice and transform the life in our communities to clearly reflect Christ. The way we are now with no structure of nationhood in place to foster Christian oneness is an error that we must come to terms with, and speedily correct. This then should be our prayer even as the Lord prayed: "I do not ask on behalf of these alone, but for those also who believe in me through their word, that they may all be one; even as thou Father, art in me and I in thee, that they may be in us; that the world may believe that thou didst send me. And the glory which thou has given me I have given to them; that they may be one; just as we are one."

Holy brethren, let us ask for wisdom and understanding, for the harvest is ripe and it is time for the reapers. For the glory of God's Kingdom is to be manifested through his church and the nation of his people. God has chosen St. Croix as a first fruit and then the rest of America to begin the process of establishing justice and holiness here in the western hemisphere. The people in this country will learn holiness through the judgment that God is bringing upon this country, so let us secure the saints. Only through the Spirit of God can people of different nationalities live in harmony and peace amongst themselves, and in the church, that the Spirit of Love is to be found. God wants this nation to reflect that glory, and He is calling on us to bring it to pass. Say not in your hearts if it is the will of God it shall so be done. But rather pray that the Lord strengthens us that we may faithfully work toward the building up of this glorious Kingdom, and the showing forth of His righteousness. During the days of evil it will go well with the saints, as it went well with the children of Israel when God sent Moses to confront Pharaoh so let us not spurn this grace. With God there is no partiality, and every one will have to give account for these words, let us then not love the world, but rather rebuke sharply those forces of immorality and evil.

Finally, on a more personal note, it is my hope to be with my wife and children who live in Tampa, for the ending of March, or during the month of April. *I* feel that such a break is needful at this time, to restore strength to my body. For this work God separated me and I separated myself to pray, fast, and meditate in the scriptures, hoping to be faithful in revealing to you the mind of God. I need your help in organizing the meeting and in finding the most appropriate location for such a historic event. Those of you who have organization skills, I'm calling on you to join in this effort to employ your skills to the glory of God, remember you are serving the Lord. Also, whatever other assistance the Lord lay upon your hearts to do, *I* pray that you will do it joyfully, and willingly.

Financially, I can use some help, but most importantly I earnestly covet your prayers. Pray that God would bring us into perfect harmony one with each other, and that we will join together faithfully after we receive the witness of this revelation. Holy and beloved brethren, *I* pray that God would knit our spirits together, and cause us to stand as one man before Him. For God has invested in us all the rights, privileges, entitlements and power of the Kingdom of His Son, Jesus; that we may subject principalities and powers to the Kingdom of God, while we enjoy the fruits of His salvation. We can then say with the psalmist: "let the godly ones exalt in glory, let them sing for joy on their beds. Let the high praises of God be in their mouth and a two-edged sword in their hand, to execute vengeance on the nations and punishment on the people: to bind their Kings with chains and their nobles with fetters of iron: to execute on them the judgment written: this is an honor for all His godly ones. Praise the Lord." Brethren we know our Lord Jesus was slain and purchased for God with His blood, people from every tribe, tongue, and nation, and made us to be a Kingdom and praise to our God, "and we shall reign upon the earth." We are His Kingdom, let us then arm ourselves with these words of prophecy and gain confidence in this work. What the Lord said He will do, that He will do. The grace of our Lord and Savior Jesus Christ gives us peace, and may we have these signs overflowing in our communities: the healing of all kinds of diseases, the casting out of demons, speaking in new tongues, restoration of families, miraculous deliverance from evil, and all the wonderful things that will manifest the seal of His Spirit in us.

I, Austin, certify before the holy family in heaven, God the Father, God the Son, God our blessed Holy Mother, (Holy Ghost) that these words are true and faithful, and will shortly come to pass. The grace of our Lord and Savior Jesus Christ be with us all. In the end I can confidently say these words: God bless you America, for you are called to be blessing in the earth; God save you America for you are called to show the way of salvation to many. God help you America for you are called to help the poor; God give you peace America, that you may bring peace to the world.

Note:

It is my desire to make a ministerial directory, and your cooperation, and suggestions are more than welcome. I want to include the type of ministry, i.e., prophetic, evangelical, pastoral etc, and the type of gifts, i.e., healing, miracles, helps, government etc. Such a directory will make it easy for the ministers to call upon each others gifts, and ministry for the glory of the body. Everything that is needed for the nation is with us, we should learn to use the gifts that God has given to us for His glory. Please send me that information that we can have such a directory. Again, let us work together to take back what the devil had stolen. Brethren the war is on!

Austin

This is a reference note.

August 8, 1993
Austin Phillips
General Delivery
Christiansted, St. Croix, VI 00820

Dear Pastors/Minister of the Gospel:

Greetings in the name of Jesus, the son of God, God the Father, and God the Holy Ghost; our eternal peace, comfort and rest.

This is the last letter that I will be writing to you before I meet with you face to face. Obviously my plans to meet with you in the month of May did not materialize, my apologies for the delay. However we know that, "ALL THINGS WORK TOGETHER FOR THE GOOD TO THEM THAT LOVE GOD, AND ARE THE CALLED ACCORDING TO HIS PURPOSE." The good is that I was forced to write to you, and share in part what was given to me for you. That which I have written will serve as a reminder to you, and also as a testament against you if you fail to act upon these words. For this I do know, that you will have to give an account to him who sent me for every one of these words.

My brethren, we have little time left before the next big war. All of us will like to have peace, but the Lord spoke to me these words, "There will be no peace, prepare for war." Some of you may say there are many wars taking place today. What does that have to do with us? The war you are to prepare for directly involves Christians, because Islam will rise and attack not only Israel, but also the so-called Christian West.

It is your sons and daughters who will be on the front line and this country will be in the forefront of the battle. You are charged with crying out against immorality, and abominable practices, and cause righteousness to bear fruit in the land.

The amount of destruction and death incurred during that war will depend on how soberly you take these words, and prepare the people. The Church of the living God will come forth victoriously, but you must prepare the people, and be prepared to fill the void of a corrupt government with responsible leadership. God will establish a Government on this earth before Jesus returns, and he is calling you to be the care takers of that Government. The church will unite and prosper. Please don't attempt to fight against God's program.

My hope is that you are not taking these words and casting them aside, but that as ministers you are sharing them with responsible people, who are able to act upon them. The blood of those whom you serve be upon your conscience, and your hands. I, Austin Phillips, have delivered to you that which has been given to me for you. I am free from your blood. The grace of our Lord and Savior Jesus Christ be with you all.

Yours in Christ,
Austin Phillips

Austin Phillips
Tampa, FL 33624
October 29, 1993

Dear Ministers:

Greetings in the name of Jesus, God the Father, God the Son, God the Holy Mother, our eternal peace, comfort and rest.

I gathered you here today to deliver to you this message from God, the Father of our Lord and Savior Jesus, the Lamb of God that takes away the sins of the world. The time for the manifestation and revelation of His word, with the demonstration and distribution of the Spirit from on high as promised by his Son, Jesus, is come. This is a time for us to share the awesome power, and glory he had reserved in heaven for the Church, the Body of Christ. This generation has been blessed to receive the promises that were written and spoken of long ago by men of God, and His Son Jesus.

Today, I urge you through the Spirit of God to prove the Spirit, to test these words, for they are words that will come to pass in your day, witnessed by your generation, and spoken by the generations after you. Those who believe will partake in the blessings that God has in store for us. Those who don't believe and refuse to obey will see it, but will not receive of the heavenly promise. These promises are true and he who is faithful will perform these words to the church, beginning this day of gathering with you, the faithful and called. He sent me with words of warning as well as instructions as to how you are to prepare for the evil ahead. He sent me to declare to you the Kingdom of God and the time of its coming forth in the flesh, and how you are to safeguard the children of the kingdom from the evil that awaits them.

Today, we find on these shores of America, a nation where the church and the state are governed by separate laws. The state laws have power over the laws of God and the Faith we follow. The state laws reign supreme in the land. How can we serve two masters? How long will we continue to deceive ourselves, and call evil, good, and good evil? By their fruits you shall know whether it is good or bad. Consequently, we see fruits of death: rampant violence, abortion, immoral sexual practices, abominable immorality, and innumerable evils which God commanded us not to let flourish in our midst. Those behaviors lead to: the destruction of the divine model of the family, the breakdown of law and order, as well as the spread of multiple diseases, some yet unheard of, to spread and destroy this nation. Those are some of the consequences of life under the current laws: Laws that do not honor the Word of God, but are contrary to it; Laws that protect and promote evil, and deliver lawbreakers from prosecution. These laws protect criminals and offer them no meaningful rehabilitation when incarcerated. Look and see, do you think that God has called us to this? No, God did not call us to be in subjection to such lawlessness.

Today, God is calling us to break the yoke of such bondage that is leading the people to death. My brethren, all unrighteousness are sin, and sin is not God. We know the wages of sin is death, but God did not call this nation to death, but to life, a life of power and glory. If the wicked rules over the righteous through laws of unrighteousness, will not the righteous be tempted to put forth their hands to evil? We know God is angry with the wicked every day, should God not be angry with us? Why, because we allow iniquity to flourish in our midst and allow the nation to be subjected to laws that protect iniquity? Our sins and sins of the nation are like stumbling blocks in our way, so we cannot put off the evil that sin brings.

How can the righteous build when there is no foundation to build upon? "If the foundation be broken down what can the righteous do?" However, "Blessed is the nation whose God is the Lord, the people whom he has chosen for his own inheritance." God has called us to be His inheritance in this land, given to His, people the church. We are called to represent God and His Holy nation. These lands of the United States of America and the whole of America is given to the church, the people of God. It should never be that the laws that uphold iniquity rules over the children of God. Lawlessness and perversion should not be allowed to flourish in America. You ministers are called to change the attitude, and character of the people of the land. We are God's chosen vessels that will be used to bring about that transformation. We then must, with all boldness, exercise ourselves in the Word of God and the faith by which we stand. Therefore let us look to heaven from where we receive the laws and commandments of life and peace. We also look to heaven to receive the promise of the heavenly gift, the Spirit of truth that will guide us in all truth. God did not call us to be weak, but to be strong and to be very courageous, exercising ourselves in the truth with all boldness.

Today, more than ever, there is a need for clarification, and a correct interpretation of the Word of God. The Church of the living God must come into harmony with the truth and will of God, and God is calling you first who shepherds the flock, to be in a state of oneness. You then will, by example, bring harmony to the rest of the body. The unity of the body rests with those who instruct the body, and we recognize now more than ever the need for unity, this need, and the call for unity has brought us here today. "This is the day that the Lord has made, let rejoice and be glad in it." This is a day in which a seed will be planted, a seed that will grow into a great nation, which will bear fruits of righteousness, unity and peace. This nation of people to be born will come forth through your obedience, for God is calling you ministers of this generation to give evidence of His truth, by manifesting the power from heaven in the Body of Christ. The world is going on in darkness, and the church, the light of the world, is called to lead the nations to paths of life and peace. The lord is calling for the unity of the Body of Christ to demonstrate to the world how people live as a nation, when they abide by the word of God and the power of His Holiness. We are called to abide faithfully to the word of God and to have a common faith, share a common baptism, and be all filled with the Spirit from heaven.

We are called to have a fervent love one for another and to gladly shine for God. We are chosen vessels suited to receive the glory of his Kingdom that will be fully manifested through us, so that we can be the true light of the world and the glory of all Kingdoms, a royal priesthood, a peculiar people His Majestic Saints on the earth.

It is truly a great honor for me to be allowed by God to be a part of this great work, a work that has a definite beginning and points to a clear ending. We know where God is taking us, we know how we are to get there, and we know what we will receive when we get to the end of our journey that God is calling us to walk; along with the Holy Family in Heaven, and the heavenly host. We are called to be a nation of high moral and ethical standards, a land of enlightened people, a people who know God, a great people. Instead we are scattered with everyone going his/her own way. This leaves the body abused, oppressed and exploited. We are victims of deceitful men and women who take advantage of the flock because of the current disorganized condition of the leadership. Where one suffers, all suffer, so let us bring under subjugation our individual desires, to the will and Word of God.

Each of us is to contribute from what we have received from God, so that no part of the body will be left out, or lacking in anything. When we live in accordance to His will, the nation of just and upright people who delight themselves in the Lord, is what people will call us. To think that we have been called to do great things through this fellowship with God does not overwhelm me as much as the knowledge that we will live and reign with him throughout eternity.

It is a great vision that the Lord revealed to me about the church in America, and the people of this island, and the rest of the United States of America in particular. For from here is where that fire will go forth, the fire that will set ablaze the entire United States and the whole of America, filling it with the knowledge of God, and the power of His Christ. There had never been such a nation, a nation of people all filled with the power of God, one that abides by the laws of God, a people who will magnify the law and make it honorable in the sight of the nations.

Let me begin with the vision God gave me for the church on St. Croix. The faithful will come together, and the spirit of God will be poured out upon them. Like a fire that spreads in a forest of dry trees with the winds to drive it on, so this gospel will spread and set the course to permanent global changes. For the nations of the world will eagerly watch to see what God is doing with us, and in the end will want to join themselves to us. The poor, the oppressed and downtrodden will shout for joy because in us they will see salvation and the hope of a better life.

The church will first go through a rapid period of growth. This will happen so suddenly, this spontaneous desire by Christians and righteous people all over the U.S. and St. Croix to bring about a Godly change will take people by surprise. The coming together of the citizens in such great numbers to answer that call will be phenomenal. Though the rise of the church will be rapid and glorious, there will come a time of trouble and difficulty. The time of reconciliation and prosperity will be brief, for the Lord will do a quick work in laying the foundation of the nation to come and the people will have a mind to work. Then the work will be stopped and the church brought low. This is a time that will affect the world entirely; it is a time of war, hatred, and devastation. A time when evil will abound and iniquity will spread itself. For the church, it will be a time of purging, a time where the worthless shepherds will be removed or will abandon their flock. A time where iniquity will be purged from the church and the mouths of liars be put to silence. The church will go through a great transformation during the time of darkness and make herself ready as a bride without spot or blemish. For the ungodly it will be a time of evil, and men will flee to the sanctuary because of the evil plague that the Lord is sending amongst men.

The church will become actively involved in every area of human life. From its struggles to bring about justice and peace and its courage to stand for moral uprightness, a people will be formed. A people who will delight to do what is right and that will trust in the power of God to help them in all things, for God will reveal himself mightily through us. The struggles and the fire of affliction will do the church good, for it will open the eyes and the ears of the people to the truth as they see the power of God. The people will respond to the call to holiness and will go and attempt to peacefully change the government so that it will be in harmony with the will of the people to be governed by the government of

Christ and the laws handed down from heaven. This will lead to attacks against the body by those who oppose godliness. The church will not be afraid to stand in the evil day because God is with us and assures us of the victory of good over evil. As an instrument of God, the church will lead justice to victory, but only through an all out effort on the part of its members. Changes in global conditions will also take place rapidly. What once appeared to be unshakable, we will see crumbling. Those who were least regarded we will see rising.

Those who appeared to be lifelong friends we will see become mortal enemies. Waves of people will get involved leading to mass demonstrations, riots, and reckless carnage. The people of God will be led out of such darkness through a life of faithfulness and dedication on the part of the saint. You, the shepherds, are to guide God's people with integrity and skillfulness, being vigilant in looking out for the believers. For the united church will become the dominant voice in the community, and be a securer of many, as it moves to break the oppressive yolks and remove the heavy burdens.

It is not going to be an easy walk, but this is a fight for our faith, our children, our nation, our wives and family, and even our very lives. For the wicked who hates, the righteous will seek to slay them, and remove them from the land. These will be difficult times, really hard times. However, we have this assurance; God will neither leave us, nor forsake us.

You, ministers, are to be the confident hands on the helm of the ship in the midst of troubled seas that the Lord will use to safely guide His people. So let us be prepared to stand with authority and courage, for the battle is upon us. We must maintain a state of peace and oneness amongst the different ethnic and cultural groups in the body: Knowing that we are to treat each other with dignity and respect, living like brothers in spite of our ethnic differences.

To add to our internal conflicts, the external forces of Islam will also rise against the Christians in the West. This will give the church more reasons to seek God's guidance. For I bear witness that Islam as a political and religious force will unite Arabs and non-Arabs under the banner of Islam. This they will do, because God will place it in their hearts to do. For God will use them as an instrument for correction against the hypocritical people who claim to know God, but does contrary to His Word. For a time they will prosper, and Jews and Christians will go through their afflictions of corrections. When God completes His work on us, this new nation here in the United States, will come forth and will lift the standards offered by Islam. By embracing Christ, and abiding by His word, we will no longer only talk about the Word, we will live it. We will not only talk about the power of God's Holy Spirit, we will demonstrate it. From the least to the greatest, everyone will know God; it will truly be a peculiar nation, a nation worthy of praise. Here in America, the land of the Christ like sons and daughters of God; there will be a spiritual people in a land flowing with milk and honey. This Man Child who is to be born in this wilderness of darkness will come to birth under stressful conditions. This is the one that will rule all nations with a rod of iron, and bring justice to the nations.

This will be a land of miracles, and healings, a land free from oppressive demons, a land well maintained and blessed by God, a land of abundance and favored by God. The nations of the world will look to this nation to settle disputes and to see things in their right order. Yes, there is great promise of blessings and glory for the people of God in America and the time for them to receive it is now. I have great confidence that once you ministers receive the witness by the Spirit of God that these words are true and faithful, that you will do according to these words and bear much fruit.

Finally, I saw in the vision how the people will live Godly lives and obey the voice of those who looks after their soul. This work is well worth the effort on our part, for I know that God will do His part. Continue in faithfulness, and may the Lord Bless us with all wisdom and understanding in the revelation of His Son, our hope and glory. The Grace of our Lord and Savior Jesus Christ be with us always.

Yours in Christ
Brother Austin Phillips

The United States Today

The United States today is one of the most prosperous nations on the earth and is inhabited by people from just about every country in the world. When the Founding Fathers established this nation, knowingly or unknowingly, they made the God of Israel the corner stone. Its principles were built upon Biblical law. The symbols and the meaning of things might appear coincidental, but God brought to this nation a group of people who were determined to be free and to serve God without fear. As time progressed, on every coin and bill were written these words, "In God We Trust." Was that coincidental or were the builders directed by God? They were led by God. For "there is a spirit in man, but the inspiration of the Almighty giveth them understanding" (Job 32:8). Also, "a man's heart deviseth his way, but the Lord directs his steps" (Prov 16:9).

Going back to the two nations that were formed together from Daniel's first beast, the United States and the western governments are the first ones we will examine. They are the inheritors of the lands of Manasseh and Ephraim who received the promise of being richly blessed. These make up the kingdom of the house of Joseph. The house of Joseph, Moses prophesied, was to be mighty and overflowing with wealth. His bounty is to be such that they would overflow and make others rich through their abundance. This people when following after righteousness, the Lord promised to prosper them and make them great. However, they turned from the true God and forsook God, bringing upon themselves the judgments that are written in his law.

God's promise to Abraham was extended to all nations of the earth through our Lord, Jesus Christ. The United States was chosen by God to establish justice and liberty throughout the earth. However, before it can effectively fulfill that calling, it must be made new. Whom the Lord loves he disciplines to deliver their soul from hell, "withhold not correction from the child: for if thou beat him with the rod, he shall not die but thou shall beat him with the rod and shall deliver his soul from hell" (Prov. 23:13-14). God will use the rod of correction and fully establish his laws and purpose unto this nation. Seeing that the United States and its inhabitants have found favor with God from their beginning, not because of their works, but because of his promise to Abraham and to Joseph, God will chastise them for their transgression, but not destroy them. They will pay for their sins, but they will also be established as a beacon of hope in the earth.

The punishment they will receive will turn into a blessing and a fulfillment of God's divine plan. No correction is pleasant; the effect is what really matters. "Blessed is the man whom thou chasteneth, O

Lord, and teach him out of thy law; that thou mayest give him rest from the days of adversity, until the pit be digged for the wicked. For the Lord will not cast off his people, neither will he forsake his inheritance. But judgment shall return unto righteousness: and all the upright in heart shall follow it" (Psalms 94:15). The influence of the power of God through his servants will be so great in the day when God calls America back to righteousness. During that time, the righteous will come together to stand for truth and righteousness in this country, and all those who are upright in their hearts will follow.

Before that takes place, conditions in the country will be ripe for change. The judges and politicians will continue to pass laws to stop the glorification of God. They will successfully embrace perversion and practice iniquity through unrighteous laws. As their sins multiply, so the divine plan and prophecies concerning this nation will unfold, and prophecy will be fulfilled. The righteous will cry out saying, "It is time for thee, Lord, to work: for they have made void thy law" (Psalm 119:126). Their actions make room for the fulfillment of the promise he made that he will trod down all them that err from his statutes: for their deceit is falsehood (Psalms 119:118.)

The prophet, Jeremiah, wrote about a time when God would judge the people or nations who hear his word and then turn away from it: "Therefore hear, ye nations, and know, o congregation, what is among them. Hear, O earth: behold I will bring evil upon this people, even the fruit of their thoughts, because they have not hearkened unto my words nor to my law, but rejected it" (Jer. 6:18-19). God's Word is for his children. If you are not one of his, then these words will seem like an idle tale. If you do belong to him, then these words should be like a spark to your eyes and heart, for you will understand the judgment that is coming upon all nations, including America.

This is the word of the Lord to this nation who has turned from righteousness to practice wicked works with the wicked. The Lord will send his four sore judgments upon the world. These are "the sword, and the famine, and the noisome beast, and the pestilence, to cut off from it, man and beast" (Ezekiel 14:21). The United States has been given a time when these judgments will come in force upon them. They will be affected by wars. The nations they fight will not prevail against them, but they will afflict this nation and make them weary because of wars and disasters.

Ezekiel, the prophet, warned us of what God will do to his people whom he sanctifies, for himself. "Now will I shortly pour out my fury upon thee, and accomplish mine anger upon thee: and I will judge thee according to thy ways, and will recompense thee for all thine abominations. And mine eye shall not spare, neither will I have pity:

I will recompense thee according to thy ways and thine abominations that are in the midst of thee; and ye shall know that I am the Lord that smiteth thee. Behold the day, behold, it is come: the morning is gone forth; the rod hath blossomed, pride hath budded. Violence is risen up into a rod of wickedness" (Ezekiel 7:8-11). Therefore, they shall have "the sword without, and the pestilence and the famine within: he that is in the field shall die with the sword; and he that is in the city, famine and pestilence shall devour him" (Ezekiel 7: 15).

Dreams about the United States of America

The following are some of the prophecies I saw concerning the United States. I offer these visions because they clearly explain how the United States connects to the first beast as described in the book of Daniel, and what role the United States plays in the revelation of the first seal, as described by John, in the book of Revelation. Some of my visions for America are good, very promising, but some of them are not encouraging. When the people of the United States accept the covenant of God to be His people, to accept Him as their God, then He will bless this nation unlike any other nation on the face of the earth. God will fulfill in America that which he spoke to the children of Israel by Moses. "Now therefore, if ye will obey my voice indeed, and keep my covenant, then ye shall be a peculiar treasure unto me above all people; for all the earth is mine: and ye shall be unto me a kingdom of priest, and a holy nation" (Exodus 19:5-6).

The Time of Darkness

These are some of the visions and revelations I received about the United States. In one dream, I saw the nation looking like a great house firmly planted on the top of a mountain. Then it gradually began sliding off of the side of the mountain. As it was sliding downward, suddenly there was a great turnaround and the nation was miraculously restored on the mountain. During that miraculous turnaround, the United States prospered and gained more than before. However, just as the prosperity peeked, it started to crumble because it was built on a weak foundation that broke under the weight.

In another vision, I saw the nation as a man climbing a ladder with the top of it going into heaven, but as he reached the top, he began to fall and kept falling. At this time, the nation will hit its lowest social, economic, and political points. This will be the worst period in the nation history. That was confirmed in another dream. The Lord showed me the land of the United States in the likeness of a great tree with green leaves. During the vision, as the leaves began to turn brown, I saw spirits descending from heaven to rest in the tree. The spirits devoured all of the leaves, green and brown, to the extent that branches, even the bark of the tree, were left very dry.

Then I saw in another vision, similar to the one before, this country and its fields were green, and the land looked prosperous. After that, I saw evil and wicked spirits descending upon the land. Then they spread throughout the land bringing famines and diseases unknown to medical science. Their rampage and destruction made the land dry and parched. It was a time of phenomenal drought. Even the evergreen trees dried up, and the grassy fields turned to dust. The rivers also dried up, and what remained was like patches of mud.

The drought, in my vision, was so severe in the United States that it negatively impacted the entire western world. Shelters were set up by the church, but supported by government, to help feed and house the people of the land. Everything was rationed. The hardship upon the land brought on great escalation of crime and violence. The people of the nation turned to God for relief from the severity of His chastisement. However, I saw that even in that time of great calamity, God provided for the faithful Christians, and they were a blessing and a light in the land.

This was not only a time of terrible drought, but also a time filled with other natural disasters such as floods, fires, earthquakes, and hurricanes. God used these natural as well as man-made disasters to plague the land. Because of the wickedness and pride of the people, terrorists attacked the nation, its people, and its interests from within and without.

I saw a time when their children glorified violence and desired it. The children showed an utter contempt for life, making the United States a dangerous place to live in. In the poor areas and the so-called ghettos, the people were not able to sleep at night because of the tension brought on by the fear of the violence from bands of criminals.

There will also come a time of extreme social tension between the various races and religious groups, leading to riots and, in some cases, outright war. That will prompt the military to patrol the streets and institute martial law to secure peace. The weak economy will be as fuel thrown on a fire. It created a frustrated, hungry, and angry citizenry. It also created a hunger and longing to bring the nation back to God and civility. The wicked hated the righteous, but the righteous contended with the wicked as the righteous fought to restore dignity and honor to this nation. The righteous strove to restore moral and prudent laws, but

the wicked sought to add iniquity to sin by desiring more immoral laws
that led to the corruption of the nation. This led to mass demonstrations
and civil unrest. The country headed toward anarchy as plague after
plague and economic hardship confronted the nation.

The Time of War

The nation was involved in one war after another. They fought
overseas to stop the nations of the east from overrunning the west. There
were four significant wars that I saw. The first three will involve Islamic
nations. The last big war before a time of peace will involve many nations.
Stirred by the Spirit of God, the righteous will not continue to take a
back seat. They will join together to fight for the salvation of this nation.
This country does not belong to the wicked, and they will not prevail
in their attempts to rule and control it. There will come a time when
lawlessness and immorality will get to the point of near anarchy, and
God will bring upon them the spirits that I saw. Fulfilling that which the
scripture says, "He turneth rivers into a wilderness, and the water springs
into dry ground; a fruitful land into barrenness, for the wickedness of
them that dwell therein" (Psalms 107:33-34).

Who will the Lord raise up against the evil doers? Who will He cause
to stand up for Him against the workers of iniquity? The Lord will use
nations from the east to punish those in the west. I saw how this nation
went to war in the Middle East and fought against the nation of Iraq, and
those nations that will support Iraq. During that war, the U.S. economy
will collapse, and the dollar will spiral downward out of control, causing
economic hardship throughout the western world and civil strife at
home. The war against Iraq is only the beginning of war in the Middle
East. The other wars will include Iran, and finally, there will be a war
against a host of Islamic nations that will join together with Egypt as their
head, that will fight against the west. This will be a bloody and costly war,
but nothing in comparison to World War Three.

The Islamic Christian wars that will come about because of America's
policies toward Islamic nations will affect the relationship between
Muslims in this country and their Christian counterparts. Only the
church through her wisdom will neutralize that tension, acting as
a buffer between racial and religious groups. The church will be the
peacemakers, the children of God.

For several critical years, the west will be plagued by those Islamic
nations, pestilence, and famines, some severe shortages of water and
food, and economic and social hardship. This affliction will be light when

in comparison to what is yet to come. What the heathens will experience when God chastises them will be much more severe. This period is not the end, nor the day of the Lord, but a shadow of what is coming, for the day of the Lord is very dark.

During this period of darkness, I saw how this great nation fell hard. The sound of its fall will resonate throughout the world because its military will be caught in a trap sprung on it by nations that will conspired against it in the Middle East. These will rise up against it suddenly when they least expect it. Their enemies will strike at them with fury and vengeance. The call to change the nation back to God in truth will be strengthened by the calamities and tribulation that God will bring upon them. In their distress, even some of their Spanish-speaking neighbors will turn against them. I saw coming from the borders in the south, armies crossing the borders to invade the nation. The saints will cry out to God, and he will hear them from his holy mountain and deliver them from their calamities.

Even some of their European allies will turn against them and forsake them. God will turn their hearts from favoring them, along with His other judgments to humble them. The way of the wicked is an abomination unto the Lord, "but he loveth him that followeth after righteousness." Upon the wicked, he shall rain snares, fire and brimstone, and a horrible tempest. This shall be the portion of their cup. "For the righteous Lord loveth righteousness; his countenance doth behold the upright" (Psalm 11:6). "The wicked shall be turned into hell and all who forget God" (Psalms 9:17), and there is neither partiality nor favoritism with God. Every man shall bear his judgment!

I saw Christians stand up and, through their spiritual convictions; bring change in the nation by changing the Constitution and the very laws that govern the land. These constitutional changes reflected the laws of God. The greatest transformation will first take place in the church, especially among the young. In those days, they will fight with every spiritual weapon in their arsenal and do everything that is legal to bring this nation back to God. God also will work with them, with mighty signs and wonders being revealed from heaven. As he did before, he will bear them witness with signs, wonders, and gifts of the Holy Ghost, showing a clear difference between those who are His and the children of wickedness whom He will plague. For the scripture says that God "repayeth them that hate him to their face, to destroy them: he will not slack to him that hate him, he will repay him to his face" (Deut.7:9-10). God will punish the wicked for their sins.

The saints will know in that day that God is with them, for he will show himself strong on their behalf. They will turn to him with their whole heart and put away their abominations and their filthiness. "Know therefore that the Lord thy God, he is God, the faithful God, which keepeth covenant and mercy with them that love him and keep his commandments to a thousand generations." It will be a fight from within for the soul of America, and a fight without for freedom and justice throughout the world.

America will be the greatest missionary battlefield ever, for Christians living in the west. They will fight to save the nation and the western world from sin and lawlessness and to take it back from the power of Satan. The forces of darkness will not succeed in turning the people away from the truth. The saints will win because "the Great, the Mighty God, the Lord of hosts, Great in counsel, and mighty in work, as a mighty terrible one will show himself to be God on their behalf. He is the God of all flesh, is there anything too hard for him to do?" (Jeremiah 32:18-19, 27).

The people cried out to God, and God stretched out His hand and saved them. The saints will triumph in changing the laws to reflect the laws of God. Through grace, and divine power, the nation began to climb again the steps leading to heaven. When it reached the top, the foundation was not weak as on the first occasion. With God's help, it continued in God's way and did not fall again, but I saw how its ships went from port to port offering protection and security to people around the world. The nation was as the police, guarding and protecting people's rights.

Daniel said he saw the beast with eagle's wings, and the wings were plucked before it was lifted up from the earth, and a man's heart given to it.

A man's spirit will be given to the inhabitants of this land. A spirit of justice and uprightness will be given to the nation. Remember, man was created in the image of God and God will pour out His Spirit upon this nation first, as He raises this nation above other nations to execute righteousness in the earth.

America must first fall and be humbled before it is permanently changed. Then I saw the evil spirits cast out of the land, through the power of the Holy Ghost, poured out on the saints who will establish God's laws as the laws, that will govern this land. At that time, God will do to them as he said he would do to Israel: "And the Lord will take away from thee all sickness, and will put none of the evil diseases of Egypt, which thou knowest, upon thee; but will lay them upon all that hate thee" (Deut.7:15).

This should be no marvel to cast evil spirits out of a country. This power is in the body of Christ to perform spiritually, and it was given to Israel to remove the wicked from among them, so as not to be entangled with them. From the Gospel of Mark, we read how a man with a legion of devils was delivered from them, and they asked Jesus not to send them out of the country. They opted to be sent into the herd of swine. The saints can and will cast those devils of hate and every wickedness out of this country.

One example is when Philip went down to Samaria and preached Christ, and the people with one accord gave heed to the things that

Philip preached; unclean spirits were cast out, crying with loud voices, the lame were healed, and those diseased people were made well. By the hands of the apostles, many signs and wonders were done, people came bringing sick folks, and them who were vexed with unclean spirits, and they were healed every one (Acts 8:7; 5:12, 16).

I saw how throughout the continental United states, different states were changed one after the other as the fire of spiritual renewal and revival swept the country. However, out on the West Coast, California was not changed. Then I saw from out of the sky what looked like a missile struck California. Also, what appeared to be an earthquake of great magnitude from the Almighty struck the West Coast. A piece of the coast was broken off and fell into the sea, killing those who lived there.

The prophetic events will be spread out over time in increments of sevens. However, great economic prosperity will proceed the brutal years. In their prosperity, they will soon forget God and turn to do evil. Then will follow the darker days that I wrote about earlier: brutal, relentless and cruel, in order to fulfill what was written by Daniel about the first beast. After those years, they will repent and be fully converted. Then will God choose them to be his peculiar treasure as he covenanted with Israel. "Now therefore, if ye will obey my voice indeed, and keep my covenant, then ye shall be a peculiar treasure unto me above all people, for all the earth is mine: And ye shall be unto me a kingdom of priest, and a holy nation" (Ex.19:5-6). Then will he pour out His Spirit upon them and glorify them.

Thank God for Jesus whose blood was shed as propitiation for our sins, and for our justification. In Jesus is the only hope for America. The natural disasters, and plagues, will come as the land seeks to purge itself from the sins of the people. The laws as I saw will be changed to reflect the laws of God, and the core of the constitution will remain, but some parts were shattered in tiny pieces. The people will turn to God in truth. The Lord will open their eyes and turn them from darkness to light, and from the power of Satan unto God, that they may receive forgiveness of sins and inheritance among them who are sanctified by faith that is in Jesus (Acts 26:18). "For God had not called us unto uncleanness, but unto holiness. "He therefore that despiseth [this word], despiseth not man, but God, who hath also given us his Holy Spirit" (1 Thessalonians 4:7-8).

Prophetic Similitudes

We read from Jeremiah that God will begin his judgment with Jerusalem, and the Christian west will naturally be drawn into the conflicts in the Middle East. The United States, as one of the nations that God has chosen to execute judgment upon other nations, symbolically is represented like the tree that Nebuchadnezzar saw, which was cut down, and he himself driven away from man.

So likewise will the United States fall and be driven from its high position.

It should be noted that Nebuchadnezzar, king of Babylon, praised and worshiped the God of heaven, and issued the following decree after Babylon was restored to him, "That every people, nation, and language, which speak any thing amiss against the God of Shadrach, Meshach, and Abednego shall be cut in pieces, and their houses shall be made a dunghill; because there is no God that can deliver after this sort" (Daniel 3:29). So likewise, as was revealed to me, will the United States and the western world will accept Jesus as Lord after they fall and are restored to an even greater glory. These will defend the Judeo-Christian faith, the foundation of their government. They will fight for the rights of the poor and needy and deliver the oppressed in their cause for truth and righteousness.

After the period of prosperity and the growth in the west, pride will overtake the government of the United States, as it did the king of Babylon. It will exalt itself against God and ascribe its glory to the workings of men. A similar decree will be issued from heaven for the United States. The United States will be like Nebuchadnezzar Babylon of which he said: "Thus were the visions of mine head in my bed; I saw, and behold a tree in the midst of the earth, and the height thereof was great. The tree grew, and was strong, and the height thereof reached unto heaven, and the sight thereof to the end of the earth: the leaves thereof were fair, and the fruit thereof much, and in it was meat for all: the beast of the field had shadow under it, and the fowls of the heaven dwelt in the boughs thereof, and all flesh was fed of it." This is how the United States will be before its great fall: feeding, protecting, defending, and supporting the nations of the world while sitting as chief amongst them.

Nebuchadnezzar continued and said, "I saw in the visions of my head upon my bed, and behold, a watcher and a holy one came down from heaven; he cried aloud [he prophesied], and said thus, 'Hew down the tree, and cut off his branches, shake off his leaves, and scatter his fruit: let the beasts get away from under it, and the fowls from his branches: Nevertheless, leave the stump of his roots in the earth, even with a band of iron and brass, in the tender grass of the field; and let his portion be with the beasts in the grass of the earth: Let his heart be changed from man's and let a beast's heart be given him; and let seven times pass over him.'"

This period of plagues that I saw coming upon this nation, turning the green leaves into dry wood and bringing in a time of social unrest and economic hardship. I described earlier. The nation fell, yet it was not totally destroyed. Even during the wars that the nation will go through, as I saw, they got a bloody nose and their pride was hurt, but they were not severely beaten nor totally cast down. Also, I saw in a related dream, how a number of nations came against the United States, and Israel. They caused damage to the nation but did not destroy it.

After all its tribulations, as I saw, the nation came out stronger, and as a holy nation because of the role of the church, lifting the standards, and teaching the people to live by faith in the Word of God. This period of judgment was foreordained by God as spoken through his prophets, as they were moved by the Holy Ghost, as is written, "This matter is by the decree of the watchers, and by demand by the word of the holy ones: to the intent that the living may know that the Most High ruleth in the kingdom of men, and giveth it to whomsoever he will, and setteth up over it the basest of men." (Dan.4:10-17).

So the nation will first go through a growth phase and, through pride, will lift itself up. God will abase them and bring upon them the evil spirits of His judgment for seven years. Then after those seven years are over, the nation will go through a seven-year rebuilding phase. At the end of that seven-year period, the nation will be given a heart of flesh and go upright or walk uprightly before God, giving Him the glory and the praise for the blessings that He had bestowed upon this land of milk and honey. Then like Nebuchadnezzar, they will say, "Now I, Nebuchadnezzar, praise and extol and honour the King of heaven, all whose works are truth, and his ways judgment: and those that walk in pride he is able to abase" (Dan. 4:37).

The Lord will use the United States to execute his vengeance upon the heathen after it is converted. Jeremiah describes the intent of the Lord for nations of the world saying: "The Lord will roar from on high, and utter His voice from His holy habitation; He will roar mightily against His fold. He will give a shout, as those who tread grapes, against all the inhabitants of the earth. A noise will come to the ends of the earth. For the Lord has a controversy with the nations; He will plead his case with all flesh. He will give those who are wicked to the sword, saith the Lord. Thus saith the Lord of Host, Behold, evil shall go forth from nation to nation, and a great whirlwind shall be raised up from the coast of the earth. And the slain of the Lord shall be at that day from one end of the earth even unto the other end of the earth: they shall not be lamented, neither gathered, nor buried; they shall be dung upon the ground. Howl, ye shepherds, and cry; and wallow yourselves in the ashes, ye principal of the flock: for the days of your slaughter and your dispersions are accomplished; and ye shall fall like a pleasant vessel. (Jer. 25:30-34). War will certainly come during the seventy years that is referred to as the end time. However, the things concerning the United States and the other nations of the world must first be fulfilled.

Likewise as Peter said that judgment must first begin at the house of God, so all the hypocrites and liars, and false teachers in the church in the west will feel the vengeance and the wrath of God upon the wicked. Likewise, the Jews at Jerusalem will feel the wrath of God as He begins His cleansing work. The Holy Ghost through mighty signs and wonders will gather many into the body of Christ. The people who are righteous will take a strong stand against the policies and immorality of the western government. This will bring about division and confrontation between the righteous and the wicked. Those in power will refuse to hear the voice of those crying out against their unlawful acts, moving God to punish the nations for their wickedness.

God will now do to the United States government and those of Europe, including Israel, what he did to Pharaoh and Egypt. A seven-year period of decay will follow the period of growth. God will bring disaster and plagues upon these nations, the likes of which they have not yet seen nor heard. So terrible will be the chastisement upon the wicked and these nations to whom the house of Joseph and Judah have come that they will seek the Lord with all their heart and mind. The Christians even though persecuted will be preserved miraculously, for they will take heed to the word of the Lord, which he had sent to warn them and prepare for the evil to come. Also, God will make a difference between the righteous and the wicked.

For Moses said, "So that the generation to come of your children that shall rise up after you, and the stranger that shall come from a far land, shall say, when they see the plagues of that land, and the sickness which the Lord hath laid upon it; and the whole land thereof is brimstone, and salt, and burning, that is not sown, nor beareth, nor any grass groweth therein [So severe will be the famine and plagues that will come upon this nation and the wicked that lives in this country, for I saw the green fields become dry and was as dust fields. They became so dry.] like the overthrow of Sodom and Gomorrah, Admah and Zeboim, which the Lord overthrew in his anger, and his wrath. "Even all nations shall say, Wherefore hath the Lord done thus unto this land? What meaneth the heat of this great anger? Then men shall say, Because they have forsaken the covenant of the Lord God of their fathers, which he made with them when he brought them forth out of the land of Egypt: For they went and served other gods, and worshipped them, gods whom they knew not, and whom he had not given unto them: And the anger of the Lord was kindled against this land, to bring upon it all the curses that are written in this book." (Deut. 29:22-27)

Those Islamic nations that God will raise up will pursue a standard of righteousness after the law, from which the west and Judah as nations will stray. So God will fulfill His Word that He spoke through the prophets to punish their land, to Israel and to the house of Judah. After He satisfies His anger, He will bring those Islamic nations into correction. These will also come to the knowledge of salvation, for they too will seek after the God of Abraham, their father.

The first group of nations to fight against the west and Israel are those from the Middle East. The war against the United States and its allies will begin with Iraq as was revealed to me. In the desert, a trap will secretly be prepared for the USA and its allies, and they will fall into it. God will give the government of the United States into their hands\ to humble them. The United States has been going through its challenges;

however, the worst is yet to come. Those wars will be one of the reasons for the economic collapse. The military will also suffer both that of the United States and its western allies. Islamic nations, of Africa, will rise to great power and status and will support the nations of Turkey, Iraq, and Iran, the three principal Islamic nations that will wage war against the west. They will call for a holy war against Israel and the west. Syria also will join them in their fight against Israel and its western allies. These will be supported by other Islamic nations around the world. Religious wars, also call for greater religious involvement. The church will be involved on a level that will confound the nations.God had commissioned them, and it is God who will send them to fight against the people of the west and the Israel. Why?

Conclusion

The world will go through tremendous changes as the United States is faced with difficult and dark days. Islamic unity and power, both economic and military, will force the nation to view religion as a necessity for its identity and survival. The church will begin to play a leading role in preparing the nation to survive the darkness that will descend upon it. In book two, **Christ Second Coming, "A Message to the Nations,"** we will continue with what will become of the rest of the world, as we examine the prophetic events surrounding the second and third seals.

Edwards Brothers,Inc!
Thorofare, NJ 08086
11 August, 2010
BA2010223